By Ed McClanahan

The Natural Man

Famous People I Have Known

*Famous People
I Have Known*

LITTLE ENIS, 1973
(The All-American Left-Handed
Upside-down Guitar Player)

ED McCLANAHAN

Famous People I Have Known

Farrar Straus Giroux

NEW YORK

Library of Congress Cataloging-in-Publication Data
McClanahan, Ed.
Famous people I have known.
PS3563.C3397Z465   1985   813'.54   [B]   85-13137

Acknowledgment is made to the following for permission to
reprint copyrighted material: *Beechwood Music Corp.* Portions of lyrics from "Loose Talk" by Freddie Hart and Ann
Lucas. Copyright © 1954 by Central Songs, Inc. A division of
Beechwood Music Corporation. Used by permission. All rights
reserved. / *Chappell and Co., Inc.* Portions of lyrics from
"Teddy Bear" by Bernie Lowe and Kal Mann. Copyright ©
1957 by Gladys Music. All rights administered by Chappell
and Co., Inc. (Intersong Music, Publisher), and Unichappell
Music, Inc. (Rightsong Music, Publisher). From "Great Balls
of Fire" by Otis Blackwell and Jack Hammer. Copyright ©
1957 by Hill and Range Songs, Inc. Assigned to Chappell and
Co., Inc. (Intersong Music, Publisher). From "All Shook Up"
by Otis Blackwell and Elvis Presley. Copyright © 1957 by
Shalimar Music Corp. All rights controlled by Elvis Presley
Music (Unichappell Music, Inc., administrator) and Unart
Music Corp. From "Blue Suede Shoes" by Carl Perkins. Copy-
right © 1956 by Hi-Lo Music, Inc. Copyright renewed, as-
signed to Carl Perkins Music, Inc. All rights administered by
Unichappell Music, Inc. International copyrights secured. All
rights reserved. / *Milene Music, Inc.* Portions of lyrics from
"Trying" by Billy Vaughn. Copyright 1952, renewed 1980 by
Milene-Opryland Music, Inc. All rights reserved. / *Hudson
Bay Music, Inc.* Portions of lyrics from "Fever" by John
Davenport and Eddie Cooley. Copyright © 1956 by Jay and
Cee Music Corp. Copyright renewed and assigned to Fort Knox
Music, Inc., and Trio Music Co., Inc. All rights administered
by Hudson Bay Music, Inc. All rights reserved. / *Leonard
Whitcup, Inc.* Portions of lyrics from "From the Vine Came
the Grape" by Leonard Whitcup. Copyright renewed 1977 by
Leonard Whitcup, Inc.

Sections of this book appeared, in different form, in
*Esquire, Playboy, The Free You,
Conjunctions,* and *The Journal of Kentucky Studies*

This book is for the women in my life:
for Cia, for Kris and Cait and Annie,
and especially for my mother, Jess McClanahan,
who put up with it all

CONTENTS

A man said to the universe:
"Sir, I exist!"
"However," replied the universe,
"The fact has not created in me
  A sense of obligation."

—STEPHEN CRANE

ONE

Introducing...
Jimmy Sacca?

Fame is the thirst of youth.

—BYRON

LET me begin by telling myself a little cautionary tale:

A few years ago an acquaintance of mine, the poetry editor of a highly regarded Southern literary quarterly, acting on an unfortunate impulse to break from the ranks of the critics and join the artistes, assembled a list of the names of several dozens of *his* literary friends and acquaintances in the form of a sort of free-verse epic poem, with his own umpty-ump associations serving as the implied narrative. He then published the composition in his magazine, for the edification of poetry lovers everywhere.

Now, this is a nice fellow we're talking about here, and there isn't a reason in the world to question his motives in this enterprise. No doubt he intended the gesture solely as a selfless tribute to all those who had figured large in his life.

But because his line of work causes him to move in pretty fast company, many of the names that turned up on the list were, if only by comparison to the rest of us, illustrious ones—and so the whole business inevitably smacked of self-aggrandizement: *Lookit the swells I run with, Ma!* Moreover, those whose names had luster must have felt that they'd been taken advantage of, just as surely as those of us who lacked it could hardly help feeling we'd been patronized. And as poetry, this concrete ode was wanting in . . . well, call it *gist*.

In short, it simply wasn't a very good idea, and I rather hope its perpetrator never reads this, because he'd probably just as soon not be reminded of it.

Yet I knew all too well where he was coming from—for I too have hobbed and nobbed with the high and the mighty, friends, and I too have gone tripping down life's pathway dropping names like a cumbersome wood nymph scattering posies. For instance:

Happy Chandler gave me an autographed baseball in 1942. I have, in my rich and varied life, ridden on elevators with both William Styron and Jim Thorpe. James Baldwin once let me buy him a drink. When I taught English in Oregon, the Original Gidget was in my freshman composition class. In 1967 Timothy Leary met Ken Kesey in my living room. (This cosmic confluence was sponsored by the Mid-Peninsula Free University of Palo Alto, California, an institution of higher—and higher, and higher—learning, of which I was, at the time, the Department of Creative Writing.) With my own eyes I saw both Ewell Blackwell and Tom Seaver pitch no-hitters for the Cincinnati Reds, thirty years apart. My father-in-law won the Pulitzer Prize. Warren Oates once let me buy him a drink. When I taught English at Stanford, Melvin Laird's niece registered for my class one term, and Sigourney Weaver baby-sat my children. I ordained Paul Newman into the ministry of the Universal Life Church. My father was once introduced to the World's Largest Hog-Ring Manufacturer. I have spoken to Dennis Hopper on the telephone. ("Hello, man, is Leo there?" "Leo? I don't think I know a . . ." "Yeh, well, listen, man, if Leo shows up, tell him Dennis Hopper called, okay?" Click.) Waite Hoyt once let my uncle buy him a drink. I myself lived much of my ladhood in Maysville, Kentucky, Birthplace of Rosemary Clooney and Home of the World's Largest Pulley Factory.

And get this: In Maysville I knew a guy who knew a guy who'd been in the army with one of Betty Grable's ex-husbands, and this guy told my friend that Betty Grable's ex-husband used to come into the barracks drunk in the middle of the night, and grab himself by the crotch and shake it, hollering, "Awright, boys, wake up and shake the hand that shook the dork that put the pork to Betty Grable!" And one time this guy got up and shook it, Betty Grable's ex-husband's hand, and after the war my friend shook *his* hand—and when my friend told me the story, I shook my friend's hand! Applicants to shake my hand may write for an appointment.

Not to suggest, certainly, that all my acquaintances are so well connected. Indeed, I dare say that in these very pages we'll happen upon several whose greatest triumph over anonymity is in having been included in a book penned by the hand that shook the hand that shook the hand that shook the hand that shook the dork that put the pork to Betty Grable. In these instances, we'll accord them as much fame—or infamy—as their deeds would seem to merit, and trust that we've done them justice. Perhaps, like Byron, they too will awake one morning and find themselves famous.

I have even, if I may say so, achieved a certain modest fame in my own right. As a matter of fact, for a brief but intoxicating moment in literary history, I may well have been the Most Famous Unpublished Author in America. In 1961, see, during my third dismal year as an untenured instructor of prescriptive grammar at (let's call it) Backwater State College in Backwater, Oregon, going down, as it were, for the third time, clutching desperately at even the flimsiest of straws, I flashed an SOS to my muse and attempted to write my way out of this Slough of Despond. And the next thing I knew, I'd somehow scored myself both a tidy advance from a reputable—if imprudent—publisher, and a fellowship to Stanford. Then, in 1963, *Esquire* magazine devoted an entire issue to "The Literary Situation," the centerpiece of which was a massive list of all the Noted Arthurs in the land, and sure enough, there it was, my very own personal name, prominently displayed smack in the middle of something *Esquire* called, in what was surely one of the least felicitous phrases of our generation, "The Red-Hot Center." Little ole unpublished me, suddenly wallowing right in there cheek to jowl with the

biggest fish in the biggest pond of all: Mailer!
Styron! Baldwin! Salinger! Bellow! And . . .
McClanahan?

Alas, friends, though I'd made a great splash, I
was out of my depth. For despite *Esquire*'s confidence that it was hailing me, even as Emerson
greeted Whitman, at the Beginning of a Great
Career, time and events and my own inadequacy to
the task quickly conspired to return me to my rightful position as the Most Obscure Unpublished Writer
in America. Andy Warhol, as everybody knows, has
promised us a future in which we'll all be famous
for fifteen minutes. But don't vote for him, folks;
fifteen minutes isn't nearly enough.

Still and all, it must be owned that a man of such
excellent connections in high places is not likely to
be bedazzled by the common, garden-variety celebrity. So it is fitting that I open this chronicle with
an account of the hour I once whiled away with
Jimmy Sacca.

Jimmy Sacca?

Return with me now to the spring of 1952, when I
was a second-semester freshman at Washington &
Lee University, the Home of the World's Largest
Concrete Footbridge. An unhappy freshman, I might
add—an unhappy, homesick, C-minus freshman with
the ego of an oyster, the super-ego of a Latin American dictator, and the id of a boatload of drunken
sailors. The only date I'd had all semester was a blind
setup with a burly Sweetbriar freshman, a Texas oil

nabob's daughter who'd once been featured in *Life* magazine as the Youngest White Girl Who Ever Shot an African Elephant. Daunted neither by her brawn nor by her eminence, I made my move in the back seat of a fraternity brother's car—and was swiftly nailed by a lethal elbow to the brisket which completely broke my spirit. Back at W&L, I reflected bitterly on the way fame goes to some people's heads, and contemplated flinging myself off the World's Longest Concrete Footbridge.

Then came spring vacation, and I hurried home to Maysville in a powerful sweat, busting to jump into my Chevy Bel Air and fly to the arms of Doris Jane Pickerell, my high school sweetie, who was majoring in home economics at Briarhopper State Teachers' College, in order (as I supposed) to persuade me that she'd make me a nice little wife someday. Imagine my chagrin when I discovered that Doris Jane's arms were presently occupied by Briarhopper State's starting fullback, whom she'd brought home to meet her parents. So it was hello Good Times goodbye, and later for you, Doris Jane.

And that's when I thought of my old high school buddy Walter Riley. Riley, who understood about small ponds better than most would-be big fish, had matriculated down at Bowling Green Business University in Bowling Green, Kentucky, and in recognition of his perspicacity had instantly been named "Mr. Freshman Personality of BGBU." He was a BGBU BMOC, Riley had intimated when I'd seen him last; as a matter of fact, he was going out with

the former Dairy Princess of Menifee County, one
of the natural wonders on the BGBU campus. If I'd
come down to see him—and bring my car—he had
promised, he'd fix me up with some of the Dairy
Princess's well-endowed court.

Which is how it came to pass that the following
evening found me sitting in a booth in a roadhouse
called the Manhattan Towers, five or six miles outside Bowling Green, in the company of Riley and
the Dairy Princess and a scowling, cheerless dow-
ager of a girl named Ernestine Grimm, who was
the date I'd driven two hundred miles to console
myself with. Riley and I were drinking Four Roses
and Coke, and Riley had induced the Dairy Princess
to experience her maiden Screwdriver. Ernestine
Grimm had declared in no uncertain terms that
drinking was against her religion; she was having a
Nehi.

Riley, whose immediate intentions involved the
back seat of my car, was earnestly entreating the
Dairy Princess to relax and drink up; vodka, he kept
assuring her, was odorless, colorless, practically the
same as water. I, meanwhile, was plumbing the
mysterious depths of the life and mind of the vi-
vacious Miss Grimm, eventually coaxing from her
that she'd been "borned and bred right cheer'n Bone
Grin," that she was majoring in Secretarial Arts
at the BU, and that she didn't dance, it was against
her religion. Newp, she hadn't seen any good movies
lately; against her religion. I asked her which religion that was, and she said the Methodist religion,

if it was any of my bee's knees. I told her I was of
the atheist persuasion, myself—which was true;
Doris Jane had destroyed my faith in everything,
forever. But atheism was definitely against Ernestine's religion. She said she'd never met an atheist
before, and only hoped to the Lord she never met
another one. The very idea made her sick to her
stummick, she said, and if she was the Good Lord
she would smack the lips off of me for saying such
a thing. She was glad her late mother wasn't alive
to see her setting in a roadhouse with an old atheist,
because if she was she would just die.

This exchange of philosophies effectively concluded our relationship. Ernestine confined her
further observations to the black looks she directed
across the table at the oblivious Riley, the object of
whose attentions was now tiddly and giggling over
her second Screwdriver. I was at liberty to drink
my Four Roses and ponder the state of my eternal
soul—not too good, if the truth be told—and, ignoring Ernestine Grimm as studiously as she seemed
bent upon ignoring me, to fix an expression of con-
summate boredom on my face and look about me,
in order to give the other patrons of Manhattan
Towers to understand that I was above the company
I was keeping.

I found myself sitting in the middle of what might
have been, that night at least, the very cradle of
boredom. Manhattan Towers, despite its name, stood
about eleven feet tall, a squat outcropping in a vast
expanse of parking lot surrounded on three sides

by a cow pasture; it took the name from a card-
board cutout of the Manhattan skyline pasted to
the back-bar mirror. Tonight it was Dead City.
There were three or four stray males languishing
in depressed-looking postures at the bar, and two
other couples cowering like hunted things in separate
booths across the dance floor, and us, the Boresome
Foursome, and a bartender and a waitress, and that
was it. The place was a tomb; even the jukebox was
out of order.

Ordinarily, Riley had explained, there'd be a
combo playing—local boys, from Western Kentucky
State Teachers' College, across town. The Hilltoppers, they called themselves, and they always drew
a crowd. But a few weeks ago they'd gone down to
Nashville and cut their first record, and lately they'd
been making a lot of personal appearances around
Nashville to promote it. So nowadays you could
never tell when they'd show up at Manhattan
Towers. He knew the Hilltoppers personally, Riley
attested; they'd played the BGBU Frosh Mixer the
night he was crowned Mr. Freshman Personality.
It was a good record, he added; everybody thought
they were going places.

As it happened, I'd heard the song myself, on the
car radio that afternoon on my way down to Bowling
Green. A dolorous little confection called "Trying"—
"I-hi-hi-hi'm try-ing to forget you / But try as I
ma-a-ay / You're still my ev-v-very thought, dear /
Ev-v-very da-a-ay . . ."—it was rendered in a gulp-
ing, lugubrious tenor (Jimmy Sacca was the re-

sponsible party there, though I didn't know that yet)
somewhat after the manner of Johnnie Ray, with a
syrup of imitation-Ink Spot harmony poured over it.
Sticky, but good; I'd liked it right away. The group's
full name was "Billy Vaughn's Hilltoppers with
Jimmy Sacca"—and yes, we're talking about *that*
Billy Vaughn, the weary housewife's secret solace,
the same Billy Vaughn whose studio orchestra, during the 1960s, rendered up all those mood-food
albums with titles like "Music to Mop the Kitchen
Floor By." But the 1952 Billy Vaughn was an altogether different article, and "Trying," which he
wrote, was a minor but not unworthy contribution
to the genre, the "I'm so lonesome I could just spit,
sh-boom, sh-boom" school of Caucasian blues.

Of course I didn't know all that yet, either. In
fact, the most that I could be said to know right then
was that the original Four Roses had somehow pro-
liferated to eight, twelve, sixteen—and judging from
the buzz that I was getting, there must have been a
bee in every rosebud. Sometime around eleven, with
my brain afloat in blended whiskey and my back
teeth afloat in Coca-Cola, I lurched off to the men's
room, where I stood for a long time perusing the
graffiti ("What are you looking up here for?" read
my favorite. "The joke is in your hand"), until
Riley came in to see if, in the popular phrase of the
day, I'd fell in.

"Where you been?" he demanded. "I thought
maybe you'd fell in."

Introducing ... Jimmy Sacca?

"Just shakin' hands with the unemployed," I sighed, zipping up.

"Listen, Mac," Riley said urgently, "you gotta stay sober so you can drive. I've been tryin' to get Cheryl into a back seat for weeks! What's-her-name's not so bad, she's just a little . . . moody. Can't you jolly her up a little?"

If looks could kill, they'd still be scraping Riley off those men's room walls, along with the rest of the graffiti. I snarled some crapulous pleasantry at him and turned to go back out to the grim business of drinking the greatest possible amount of Four Roses in the shortest possible time.

But just as I reached for the door it swung open, and into those narrow confines strode the most impressive personage I'd had in my sights since Happy Chandler and Rosemary Clooney and Ewell Blackwell all rolled into one, an easy six-feet-four of what fan magazines would soon be describing as "a tall, dark, 'n' dangerous Latin-lover type," *big* guy, broad-shouldered and brawny, swart, with hooded eyes like Victor Mature and a Tony Curtis forelock, tough like Steve Cochran but cool like Robert Mitchum, definitely—except perhaps for a certain beefiness along the jawline, presaging a hefty middle age— matinee-idol material, a sheik, a Valentino. He was wearing, incongruously, a Western Kentucky State Teachers' College football letter sweater.

"Hiya, Personality," he said as he breezed past Riley. "Howza kid?"

Riley, steering me back across the dance floor, was all aglow with self-esteem. That, he exulted, was Jimmy Sacca. The Hilltoppers must've got back early from Nashville; they'd probably begin playing soon, and things would start picking up in the Manhattan Towers, and if I would just straighten up and keep my goddamned atheistical ass sober for a little while (Riley wasn't mincing words), why, I'd get to hear these virtuosi who were soon to set all America singing.

Too late, Riley; nice try, but too late. For by the time the Hilltoppers had wet their whistles and assembled themselves on the bandstand and begun tuning up, I had put away most of yet another dozen Roses, and suddenly I was . . . out of the question. I couldn't talk, I couldn't see, and I was pretty sure that when I tried to walk I'd find I couldn't do that, either. I had been struck dumb, blind, and halt by blended whiskey. I struggled to my feet, mumbling something about going for a li'l air, and staggered off across the wildly tilting dance floor. On the bandstand Jimmy Sacca was testing his microphone. As I stumbled and bumbled my spastic way through the crowd—for now there *was* a crowd, somehow— I heard him crack into the mike, "There goes another satisfied customer, folks! Testing, two, three, four . . ."

Riley caught up with me at the door and demanded the car keys. Outside, I tried briefly to argue with him, but whatever I said didn't make much sense even to me, so I handed them over.

Introducing ... Jimmy Sacca?

"Go sleep it off in the car," Riley ordered. "And listen, atheist"—he flung this over his shoulder as he turned to go inside—"if you puke in it, I hope God *does* smack your damn lips off!"

Blow it out yer bloomer leg, Riley, I might have told him if I could've remembered how to talk; it's my own damn car, I'll puke in it any time I want to. But Riley was already long gone, and I was reeling around all by myself in the darkened parking lot, caroming off unfamiliar fenders, barking my poor shins on bumpers and tailpipes, now on my hands and knees down in the gravel, now on my feet again . . . at last groping my way into the narrow slot between my own yellow Chevy and one of those postwar Ford sedans of that bilious hue that Doris Jane Pickerell, whose father owned one, used to call "monkey-vomit green." Then, I remember, I was stricken by an urgent and awful nausea, I was knee-walkin', commode-huggin' drunk and I was *sick*, friends, sick as a dog, sick as a poisoned crow . . . And then I must have achieved oblivion, the inebriate's satori, for that's the last thing I remember until . . .

Jimmy Sacca?

None other. Suddenly my eyes flew open like windowshades, and there was Jimmy Sacca's glowering visage hanging over me, upside down, not an arm's length away, Jimmy Sacca's great paw gripping my shoulder, shaking me none too gently from my stupor, Jimmy Sacca's mellifluous tenor, now shrill with righteous indignation, squawking:

15

"Are you the dirty dog that puked on Billy's fender?"

Ohhhh me. I squeezed my eyes shut, yet even through closed lids I saw it all: saw with awful clarity myself stretched out on my back across the car seat with my legs and feet all snarled up in some impossible Gordian knot among the floor pedals and the steering column; saw Jimmy Sacca fling open the car door and lean in to discover, ghastly in the feeble glow of the dome light, this reechy, wretched wad of human misery—for now my very eyeballs were pulsating systolically to the throbbing Latin rhythm of my headache, bulging and contracting in their sockets in time with the blood pounding in my temples—saw Sacca recoil at the disgusting spectacle that confronted him, some revolting degenerate lying right there where decent people were expected to put their nice clean rumps. Was I the dirty dog that puked on Billy's fender? I knew immediately, by the unholy taste in my mouth, that he'd got his man.

And now there was another voice (whose? This "Billy" person's? Billy who? Billy Vaughn, of course, who else? But what the hey, just because somebody had a little accident on the fellow's fender, that didn't give them the right to go around rousting peaceful citizens from their slumber, did it? I mean, if a person can't stretch out for a little snooze in his own car without a bunch of tinhorn musicians . . .), another angry voice issuing from behind Sacca's looming bulk:

Introducing . . . Jimmy Sacca?

"Yeh, what the hell are you doin' in my automobile, kid?"

His automobile? That put things in a whole new light. The first electric twitch of real panic stabbing me into consciousness, I struggled to free my legs from the impedimenta that entangled them, so I could sit up and straighten out this little misunderstanding. ("Now then, gentlemen, harrumph, now that you can see me better, it is of course perfectly apparent that a man of my obvious stature would never stoop to puking on another's fender, heh heh, certainly not, but that's quite all right, don't apologize, why don't we all just step back into my club here and allow me to buy you gents a little drink, a Four Roses and Coke for me, barkeep, and these gentlemen will have . . .")

But as I lifted my poor throbbing head above the dashboard and forced my gritty eyelids open, I saw that my darkest fears had come to pass, all of them and then some. Because not only was I sitting in someone else's car—that Ford sedan, that same old bile-green banger with the newly decorated fender— not only was I suffering a hangover of such heroic proportions that it very nearly constituted a tragedy in its own right, not only had all that come down upon me, but now I saw that the Manhattan Towers was shut down tight, its once brilliant rooftop neon sign now just a crisp of blackened script across the starry nightscape. All around us was an unbroken sea of gravel parking lot, and *my* car, my lovely little canary-yellow-and-charcoal-gray Chevy Bel Air with whitewalls and Powerglide, that I'd got for high school graduation for being the most spoiled kid in my class, was nowhere to be seen. The world I'd awakened to could not have seemed stranger, more alien, had I lain slumbering there for twenty years, like Rip Van Winkle.

At the open car door, Jimmy Sacca stood with his great arms folded across his great ex-footballer's chest, scowling down at me like something loathsome he'd discovered on his shoe sole; and beside him, aping Sacca's pose right down to the way he was impatiently drumming the fingers of his right hand along his left biceps, stood Billy Vaughn, shorter and plumper and fairer and maybe a little older than his companion, but, to a man in my condition, almost as menacing.

"Um, you men didn't happen to notice a Bel Air around here, I don't guess? Yellow and gray? With whitewalls? And Powerglide?"

"Ssssheeeit," hissed Billy Vaughn, with withering scorn.

"Well, ah, how about my buddy Walter Riley? Didn't run into him, by any chance, did you? Riley? Walter?" Sacca's scowl was utterly pitiless. "Short guy? Redheaded? Mr. Personality of BGBU?"

Sacca snorted, and raked a shoe sole through the gravel. Filled with dread, I prepared to meet my Maker—for, indeed, there are no atheists in foxholes. "The remains of an unidentified youth," tomorrow's papers would report, "beaten profusely about the head and shoulders, were found yester-

day in an abandoned parking lot near Bowling
Green . . ."

"Riley? The kid that was in the toilet? What
about him?"

"Yeh," Billy Vaughn chimed in, "what about
him?"

"Well," I ventured, encouraged ever so slightly,
"I *hope* he's got my car. I'm staying at his place,
and I kind of think I sort of remember giving him
my keys when I came outside. I guess I got in the
wrong car. I must've been a little mixed up."

Billy Vaughn was unmoved. "Must of, by God,"
he snarled, glancing at his defiled fender.

Wearily I summoned my meager reserves of
strength and will for one last assault on their sympa-
thies, one last great do-or-die extravaganza of boot-
licking and gravel-groveling ("Please, fellas!" I
could hear myself pleading as they rolled up their
sleeves to pummel me to a pâté. "I'm a sick man!"),
when, just as I was making ready to fling myself
at their feet and on their mercies, it came to me that
there was a stratagem I hadn't tried yet. I turned to
Sacca and gazed up at him adoringly, and murmured:

"Mr. Sacca, do you suppose I could have your
autograph?"

For a long moment, my fate hung in the balance.
Then, "Awww shoot, Bill," said Jimmy Sacca in that
clear, piping voice that was shortly to become his
fame and fortune, "the boy looks sick enough already. Let's give him a break."

"I'll give him a damn break," Billy Vaughn promised. "I'll break his damn leg for him, here in a minute." But he was resigned. "Well, hell," he said, "let's get him out, then."

"Uh, say there, men," I put in hastily, figuring I'd just as well be hung for a sheep as a goat, "I don't guess you men could see your way clear to give me a lift to town, could you? I mean, if you happen to be headed that . . ."

"A lift!" Vaughn marveled. "A goddamned lift! Did we take you to raise?"

I pretended not to hear him. "See, Mr. Sacca," I gushed, "the thing is, my girlfriend and I, well, you're our favorite singer and all. And it's her I want the autograph for. Because 'Trying' is, you know, it's *our* song!" This wasn't a total fiction, actually; Doris Jane Pickerell and I were definitely trying to forget each other.

"Awww shoot, Bill," Sacca drawled again, "I reckon we just as well give this old boy a ride to town, don't you?"

Vaughn stalked around to the driver's side, giving the unclean corner of the Ford the widest possible berth. Sacca dropped into the seat next to me.

"So you like my song, you say?"

"Oh yeah, you bet, Mr. Sacca!" I cried, rummaging busily through my pockets in search of a pencil and a scrap of paper. "I think it's a . . . a real smasherooney!"

Sacca whipped out his own pen and scrawled his name with an extravagant flourish across the inside of a Manhattan Towers matchbook. "Here you go, old top," he said. "Y'know, I have to keep a pen on me at all times, since my record came out."

"*Your* record?" Vaughn grunted peevishly as he settled himself behind the wheel. He peered at me in the gloom. "You're not gonna get sick on us again, are you? You don't look so damn hot to me."

"No no," I assured him, "I'm fine now." Privately, I hadn't felt so bad since the time in high school when Riley and I tried to turn a Grapette into wine by adding rubbing alcohol to it. But it wouldn't do to let my patrons know how bad off I was; they might've decided to put me out of my misery.

Vaughn started the engine and scratched gravel halfway across the parking lot. "Well, hell, all right then," he said, pausing at the edge of the highway. "Where does this Riley live?"

I drew a deep breath. "Why, uh, the thing is, I just got to Bone Grin—ah, Bowling Green today, and, uh, he lives in this boardinghouse kind of place, see, but I only stopped by there for a minute this afternoon to change clothes, and I guess I left the address in my other pants, so I kind of forget just exactly *where* it . . ." Vaughn was hunched over the wheel, gently hammering his forehead with the heel of his hand. "Uh, say there, Mr. Vaughn," I interrupted myself hastily, "I wonder if I could just get you to put your John Henry on this matchbook too? Because you know it'd just mean the world and all to my girl if . . ."

Vaughn proved even quicker on the draw than Sacca; in an instant he had his fountain pen uncapped and, squinting in the feeble light of the dash, was inscribing his signature just under his associate's. "There you go, partner," he said expansively, handing back the matchbook—my reprieve, signed in full. "I hope you and your sweetheart will get a whole lot of pleasure out of owning it, as the years go by. Now then"—he leaned forward to speak across me—"whatsay, Jimbo? I guess we could help the boy find his buddy, don't you?"

If Sacca was entertaining certain second thoughts as to the matter of my sincerity, he didn't betray them. Instead, he suggested that we proceed forthwith to the BGBU girls' dormitory, where, he said, he knew a girl who might know Riley. In no time we were tooling along through the dark, deserted streets of Bowling Green, while I, as a man of the world who'd traveled and studied widely and felt the pulse-beat of the nation, wove for my benefactors the most extravagant fabrications my weary mind could devise about the delirious enthusiasm with which "Trying" was already being received on the juke-boxes and radios of America. I smothered any lingering doubts they may have had beneath the sheer weight of my admiration, and we made it all the way to the BGBU campus without a single skeptical peep out of them.

As the Ford pulled up in front of the forbidding old red-brick dorm—which I reluctantly recognized as the same one from which Riley and I had extracted the Dairy Princess and her winsome lady-in-waiting about three weeks earlier that same evening—

Introducing ... Jimmy Sacca?

Vaughn and Sacca were listening raptly to my breathless account of the electrifying effect "Trying" had had on my wealthy, worldly peers at W&L, where, I assured them, it was held to be merely the greatest work of music since "The Washington & Lee Swing."

Sacca shushed me, and told Vaughn to turn off his headlights. "Her room's down at the end on the second floor," he said. "Pull up as close as you can, and keep the motor running."

"Roger," Vaughn said. "How you gonna wake her up? Want me to honk the horn?"

Sacca shook his head almost violently. (Those were the days, remember, when a male who got caught on the grounds of a girls' dormitory at three o'clock in the morning would have been subject to summary emasculation on the spot, by an irate housemother with a pair of pinking shears.) Even before the Ford had eased to a complete stop he was out the door and tiptoeing stealthily across the lawn toward the darkened building. He looked back once, a finger to his lips, then moved directly beneath the window he had signified. Now, limned in moonlight, he planted his feet upon the sod, raised his arms, lifted his eyes to the heavens—or at least to the second story—and crooned:

> *I-hi-hi-hi'm try-ing to forget you,*
> *But try as I ma-a-ay . . .*

Now, if there were any justice in this world, what would have happened next is that the maiden fair who flung open her window and squealed "Oooooo, Jimmmeee!" would turn out to be none other than the Dairy Princess herself, light of good old Riley's soon-to-be-foreshortened life. Then she'd let down a ladder of her hair, so that Sacca—and his pals, don't forget his pals—could scamper up and knock off an extracurricular quickie.

But that was a little too much to ask. What actually happened was simply that the girl who flung open her window and squealed "Oooooo, Jimmmeee!" (she really did) was one I'd never seen before, nor ever to my knowledge saw again. And her head was as bristly with pincurlers as a pineapple, so the old Rapunzel rappel was definitely not in the picture.

But she did know where the elusive Riley dwelt, and within five or ten minutes Vaughn and Sacca had delivered me to his door—there was my Bel Air, parked in the driveway!—and I had thanked them effusively and we had parted company, presumably forever. In the kitchen of the rooming house, I found Riley waiting up for me, and he looked so relieved when I walked in that I forgave him on the spot.

There's just one thing left to record about that most memorably forgettable of evenings: While I sat there in the kitchen recounting my adventures to Riley, I noticed him slapping his pockets for a light, and without thinking I tossed him my Manhattan Towers matchbook. The next thing I knew, Riley—who habitually neglected to Close Cover Before Striking—was frantically juggling a sulphurous yellow ball of fire in his hands, and the next after that he was grinding the charred remains of my matchbook into the linoleum with his heel, sucking his scorched thumb and crying "Dod dab muddle-fuggle madges!" Billy Vaughn and Jimmy Sacca had avenged me.

It was also comforting to learn that Ernestine Grimm had demanded to be returned to the dorm shortly after I'd executed my amazing vanishing trick, and that Riley had found no opportunity to avail himself of the lavish appointments of my back seat, or of the lavish appointments of the Dairy Princess therein.

There remains, of course, much to be told—though not by me—about the Hilltoppers. For who can forget "P.S., I Love You" or "Till Then" or "From the Vine Came the Grape" or—my own all-time favorite—"I'd Rather Die Young"? During the middle fifties Jimmy Sacca logged more radio air time than H. V. Kaltenborn, and Gold Records swirled down about the shoulders of the Hilltoppers like dandruff in a Brylcreem commercial. But in 1956 there occurred the cataclysm that called itself Elvis Presley, and hard on Elvis's heels came Little Richard and Buddy Holly and Chuck Berry and Gene Vincent and their brethren, and when the dust had cleared, the Hilltoppers—along with Guy Mitchell and Teresa Brewer and Shep Fields and His Rippling Rhythm and even Rosemary Clooney (not to mention H. V. Kaltenborn)—were effectively out of business. Billy Vaughn, as I have said, went on to become *that* Billy Vaughn; but on the airwaves of America, Jimmy Sacca's golden voice was stilled for good.

Yet we haven't seen the last of him, though we've decades to account for, and famous folk galore, before we get around to him again. In the meantime, look alive; for the world, ever on the smallish side, is getting smaller all the time, and—who knows?— maybe just around the next corner of your life, you'll come face to face with . . . Jimmy Sacca!

TWO

The Day
the Lampshades Breathed

We must all be foolish
at times. It is one of
the conditions of liberty.

—WALT WHITMAN

LIKE everybody else who lived in California during the 1960s, I Went Through a Phase. I grew me a mustache and a big wig, and got me some granny glasses and pointy-toed elf boots and bell-bottom britches (which did not, Charles Reich to the contrary notwithstanding, turn my walk into "a kind of dance"; *nothing* could turn my walk into a kind of dance). I threw the Ching. I rocked and I rolled. I ingested illicit substances. I revoluted.

But this was not my first attack of *mal de Californie*. I'd been through it all before.

By way of explanation, let me go all the way back to 1952, just long enough to say that after that uninspired freshman year at Washington & Lee, I moved on for three more uninspired years at Miami of Ohio, where I majored in 3.2 beer and blanket parties on the golf course and published uninspired short stories in the campus lit mag. In 1955, I went to Stanford, to try my hand at creational writage in graduate school.

Stanford was too many for me. I lasted just two quarters before I received a note from the chairman of the English Department inviting me to drop by and discuss my highly improbable future as a graduate student. I declined the invitation but took the hint, dropped out, and slunk back home to Kentucky to conclude a brief and embarrassingly undistin-

guished graduate career at the state university in
Lexington. Thence to Oregon, and four years of
honest toil at Backwater State College, in the freshman composition line.

But California had left its mark on me. For I had
gone West the blandest perambulatory tapioca pudding ever poured into a charcoal-gray suit, and I
came home six months later in Levi's and cycle boots
and twenty-four-hour-a-day shades and an armpit of
a goatee and a hairdo that wasn't so much a duck's-
ass as it was, say, a sort of cocker spaniel's-ass. I
had been to San Francisco and seen the Beatniks in
North Beach, I had smoked a genuine reefer, I had
sat on the floor drinking cheap Chianti and listening
to "City of Glass" on the hi-fi. I'd been Californified
to a fare-thee-well, and I'd loved every minute of it.

So when I weaseled my way back into Stanford—
and California—in the fall of 1962, via a Wallace
Stegner Fellowship in Creative Writing, it was a
case of the victim returning to the scene of the
outrage, eager for more. Immediately, I sought out
my old Stanford roommates, Jim Wolpman and Vic
Lovell, who were now, respectively, a labor lawyer
and a grad student in psychology, living next door to
each other in a dusty, idyllic little bohemian com-
pound called Perry Lane, just off the Stanford
campus. Among their neighbors was Ken Kesey,
himself but lately down from Oregon, whose novel
One Flew Over the Cuckoo's Nest had been published just a year ago and was in fact dedicated to
Vic—"Who told me dragons did not exist, then led

me to their lairs"—for having arranged Ken's enrollment as a test subject in a drug-experiment program at the local VA hospital. And the neighborhood was fairly crawling with writers and artists and students and musicians and mad scientists. It was just what I was looking for: a bad crowd to fall in with. I moved in a couple of blocks down the street, and started my mustache.

In a lot of ways, it was the same old California. We still sat on the floor and drank cheap Chianti, though now we listened to Sandy Bull and called the hi-fi a stereo, and the atmosphere was often murky with the sickly-sweet blue smaze of the dread devil's-weed. The manner we'd cultivated back in the fifties was sullen, brooding, withdrawn but volatile, dangerous—if not to others, then at the very least to ourselves. Its models were Elvis, James Dean, Marlon Brando in *The Wild One*. The idea was to seem at once murderous, suicidal . . . and sensitive.

(Locally, our hero in those days had been, improbably enough, the president of the Stanford student-body government, George Ralph, who'd campaigned in sideburns and *Wild One* leathers, behind the sneering slogan "I Hate Cops." George's campaign was a put-on, of course—between those sideburns was a dyed-in-the-wool Stevenson Democrat—but he had the style down cold, and he beat the cashmere socks off the poor Fraternity Row creampuff who opposed him.)

But six years can wreak a lot of changes, and by 1962 the future was already happening again on

Perry Lane. "We pioneered"—Vic was to write*
years later, with becoming modesty—"what have
since become the hallmarks of hippie culture: LSD
and other psychedelics too numerous to mention,
body painting, light shows and mixed-media presen-
tations, total aestheticism, be-ins, exotic costumes,
strobe lights, sexual mayhem, freakouts and the
deification of psychoticism, Eastern mysticism, and
the rebirth of hair." Oh, they *wanted* to maintain
their cool, these pioneers, they wanted to go on
being—or seeming—aloof and cynical and hip and
antisocial, but they just couldn't keep a straight face.
They were like new lovers, or newly expectant
mothers; they had this big, wonderful secret, and
their idiot grins kept giving it away. They were the
sweetest, smartest, liveliest, craziest bad crowd I'd
ever had the good fortune to fall in with. And their
great secret was simply this: They knew how to
change the world.

"Think of it this way," my Perry Lane friend
Peter, who never drew an unstoned breath, once
countered when I mentioned that my TV was on
the fritz: "Your TV's all right. But you've been
lookin' at it wrong, man, you've been bum-trippin'
your own TV set!"

For a while there, it almost seemed as if it might
really be that easy. The way to change the world
was just to start looking at it right, to stop bumming

* In *The Free You*, the magazine of the Mid-Peninsula
Free University of Palo Alto.

it out (ah, we could turn a phrase in those days!) and start grooving on it—to scarf down a little something from the psychedelicatessen and settle back and watch the world do its ineluctable thing. Gratified by the attention, the world would spring to life and cheerfully reveal its deepest mysteries. The commonplace would become marvelous; you could take the pulse of a rock, listen to the heartbeat of a tree, feel the hot breath of a butterfly against your cheek. ("So I took this pill," said another friend, reporting back after his first visit to the Lane, "and a little later I was lying on the couch, when I noticed that the lampshade had begun to breathe . . .") It was a time of what now seems astonishing innocence, before Watergate or Woodstock or Vietnam or Charles Manson or the Summer of Love or Groovy and Linda or the Long, Hot Summer or even, for a while, Lee Harvey Oswald, a time when wonder was the order of the day. One noticed one's friends (not to mention oneself) saying "Oh wow!" with almost reflexive frequency; and the cry that was to become the "Excelsior!" of the Day-Glo Decade, the ecstatic, ubiquitous "Far out!" rang oft upon the air.

The first time I ever felt entitled to employ that rallying cry was on Thanksgiving of 1962. That evening, after a huge communal Thanksgiving feast at the Keseys', Ken led me to his medicine cabinet, made a selection, and said matter-of-factly, "Here, take this, we're going to the movies." A scant few minutes later he and I and three or four other lunatics were sitting way down front in a crowded Palo Alto theater, and the opening credits of *West Side Story* were disintegrating before my eyes. "This is . . . CINERAMA!" roared the voice-over inside my head as I cringed in my seat. And though I stared almost unblinking at the screen for the next two hours and thirty-five minutes, I never saw a coherent moment of the movie. What I saw was a ceaseless barrage of guns, knives, policemen, and lurid gouts of eyeball-searing color, accompanied by an ear-splitting, cacophonous din, throughout which I sat transfixed with terror—perfectly immobile, the others told me afterward; stark, staring immobile, petrified, trepanned, stricken by the certainty, the absolute *certainty*, that in one more instant the Authorities would be arriving to seize me and drag me up the aisle and off to the nearest madhouse. It was the distillation of all the fear I'd ever known, fear without tangible reason or cause or occasion, pure, unadulterated, abject Fear Itself, and for one hundred and fifty-five awful minutes it invaded me to the very follicles of my mustache.

Then, suddenly and miraculously, like a beacon in the Dark Night of the Soul, the words "The End" shimmered before me on the screen. Relief swept over me, sweet as a zephyr. I was delivered. The curtain closed, the lights came up. I felt grand, exuberant, triumphant—as if I'd just ridden a Brahma bull instead of a little old tab of psilocybin. If they'd turned off the lights again I'd have glowed in the dark. Beside me, Ken stood up and stretched.

The Day the Lampshades Breathed

"So how was it?" he inquired, grinning.

"Oh wow!" I croaked joyfully. "It was fa-a-ar out!"

And in that instant, for me, the sixties began. Characteristically, I was about two years late getting out of the gate, but I was off at last.

Ken Kesey was, and is, a singular person, as all who know him will attest. But these were *all* singular people, this lunatic fringe on Stanford's stiff upper lip. I should probably keep this to myself, but to tell the truth, the thing I remember best about the next few years is the parties. We had the swellest parties! Parties as good as your childhood birthday parties were supposed to be but never were; outrageously good parties, parties so good that people would sometimes actually forget to drink!

The best parties were immaculately spontaneous. Typically, they began with some Perry Lane denizen sitting at the breakfast table, staring out the kitchen window into the dappled, mellow perfection of a sunny California Saturday morning, resolving: Today, I'm gonna take a little trip. By early afternoon, two or three friends would have dropped by and signed on for the voyage, and together they'd choke down either some encapsulated chemical with an appetizing title like URP–127, or an equally savory "natural" concoction like peyote–orange juice upchuck or morning-glory seeds with cream and sugar (don't try it, reader; it ain't Grape-Nuts, and there's nothing natural about it), and then for the next half hour or so they'd lie around trying not to throw up while they waited for the lampshades to start respirating. A similar scene was liable to be transpiring in two or three other Perry Lane households at the same time, and it wouldn't be long till every lampshade in the neighborhood was panting like a pufferbelly. The incipient party would have begun to assert itself.

Under the giant oak by Vic's front door—the very oak in whose shade Thorstein Veblen was alleged to have written *The Theory of the Leisure Class*—half a dozen solid citizens with pinwheel eyeballs might be banging out an aboriginal but curiously copacetic sort of hincty bebop on upturned wastebaskets, pots and pans, maybe an old set of bongos left over from the fifties, Vic himself laying down the basic bop lines on his favorite ax, a pocket-comb-and-tissue-paper humazoo. Next door at the Keseys', they'd have drawn the blinds and hung blankets over the windows, and Roy Seburn, a wonderfully hairy artist who lived, apparently on air, in a tiny box on the back of his pickup in a succession of back yards, would be demonstrating his newest creation, a rickety contraption which projected amorphous throbbing blobs of luminous color all over the walls and ceiling, like lambent, living wallpaper, to the murmuring chorus of oh-wows and far-outs that issued from an audience of several puddles of psyche-delicized sensibility on the Kesey carpet. Over at my house on Alpine Road, Peter and I were feverishly juicing peyote buttons in my wife's brand-new Osterizer.

The Day the Lampshades Breathed

In the late afternoon, Gurney Norman, another apprentice writer from Kentucky, might turn up, sprung from Fort Ord on a weekend pass. Gurney had made his way to Stanford and Perry Lane a couple of years earlier (it was he, in fact, who'd spotted the original breathing lampshade), and had then gone into the army to complete an ROTC obligation, and promptly bounced back to California in the guise of a first lieutenant, running recruits through basic training down at Ord during the week and expanding his horizons at Perry Lane on the weekends. The military was doing great things for Gurney's organizational skills; within minutes of his arrival he'd have a squad of giggling beardy-weirdies and stoned Perry Lane–style WACS in muumuus hut-hoop-hreep-hoing up and down the street with mops and broomsticks on their shoulders, in an irreverent gloss on the whole idea of close-order drill.

Eventually the party would assemble itself somewhere, more than likely around the corner at Chloe Scott's house, to take on victuals and cheap Chianti. Chloe is at all odds the most glamorous woman I've ever known. A professional dancer and dance teacher, redheaded and fiery, a real knockout and a woman of the world, Chloe Kiely-Peach of the British gentry by birth, daughter of a captain in the Royal Navy, she'd come to America, to New York, as a girl, during the Blitz, and had stayed on to become, in the early fifties, part of Jackson Pollock's notoriously high-spirited East Hampton social circle. Along the way she married a dashing young naturalist and spent a year on the Audubon Society's houseboat in the Everglades, fell briefly under the spell of a Reichian therapist and basted herself in an orgone box, and at last, divorced, made her way West to settle in as one of the reigning free spirits on Perry Lane. At Chloe's, anything could happen.

And, as they say, usually did. For starters, Neal Cassady might fall by, the Real Neal, Kerouac's pal and the prototype for Dean Moriarty of *On the Road*, trailing adoring fallen women and authentic North Beach beatniks in his wake, looking like Paul Newman and talking as if he'd been shooting speed with a phonograph needle—which, come to think of it, he probably had: "Just passing through, folks, don't mind us, my shed-yool just happened to coincide with Mr. Kesey's here, and all that redundancy, you understand, not to mention the works of Alfred Lord Tennyson and the worst of the poems of Schiller, huntin' and peckin' away there as they did, except of course insofar as where you draw the line, that is, but in any case I believe it was at, let me see, Sebring, yes, when Fangio, with the exhaust valves wide open and the petcocks too that you've sometimes seen, starting with Wordsworth, you see, and working backward, in the traditional fashion, straight through Pliny the Elder and *beyond*, though it's much the same with the fusion of the existential and the transcendental, or, if you will, the universal and the transmission, as in the case of the 1940 flat-head Cadillac 8, why, you naturally get your *velocity* mixed up with your *veracity*, of course, and who *knows* what that's cost us? So I'll just say how-d'ye-do to my friend Mr. Kesey, and then we'll be on our way, have to get there in plenty of time, you understand . . ." Neal never stuck around for long, but he was terrific while he lasted.

Then there was Lee Anderson, a roly-poly, merry little apple dumpling of a Ph.D. candidate in some obscure scientific discipline at Stanford, who could sometimes, at very good parties, be prevailed upon to . . . play himself! Bowing to popular demand, blushing bashfully from head to toe, Lee would strip down to his skivvies (an effective attention-getting device at any party), wait for silence, and at last begin rhythmically bobbing up and down to some inner tempo, as though he were about to improvise a solo on an invisible stand-up bass, now lightly slapping himself with his open hands on his plump little thighs and roseate tummy—*slappity-slappity-slappity-slap*—now cupping one hand in his armpit and flapping the arm to produce a small farting sound, like a tiny tuba—*slappity-slappity-poot-poot, slappity-poot, slappity-poot*—now shaping his mouth into an oval and rapping on his skull with the knuckles of first one hand, then the other, then both, making of his mouth a sort of reverb chamber—*pocketa-pock, pocketa-pock, pocketa-pecketa-pucketa-pock*—picking up the tempo, working furiously, sweat flying, the whole ensemble tuning in—*slappity-pock, slappity-pock, slappity-pocketa-poot, slappity-pocketa-poot, pocketa-poot, pocketa-pecketa-*

poot, *pecketa-pucketa-poot*, *slappity-pucketa-poot-poot*, *slappity-pucketa-poot-poot* . . . It wasn't the New York Philharmonic, maybe, but Lee's was a class act just the same—as Dr. Johnson might have put it, the wonder was not that he did it well, but simply that he could do it at all—and it always brought the house down.

I'm not exactly sure what Vic means by "sexual mayhem," so I won't try either to confirm or to deny it. I'll just say that during one party I opened the door to the darkened bedroom where the coats were piled on the bed and heard a muffled female voice say from the darkness, "Close the door, please, Ed. We're fucking in here."

Basically, though, the parties were just good, clean, demented fun. At any moment the front door might burst open and into the celebrants' midst would fly Anita Wolpman, Jim's wife, with the collar of her turtleneck sweater pulled up over her head, hotly pursued by Jim, brandishing an ax gory with ketchup. Or Bob Stone, a splendid writer who has also done some Shakespeare on the stage, might suddenly be striding about the room delivering himself, with Orson Wellesian bombast and fustian, of an impromptu soliloquy, a volatile, unreproducibly brilliant admixture of equal parts Bard, King James Bible, *Finnegans Wake*, and (so I always suspected) Bob Stone. Or Lorrie Payne, a madcap Australian jack-of-all-arts, might wander in with a skinned green grape stuffed halfway into one nostril and part the horrified multitudes before him like an exhibitionist at a DAR convention. Or one might find oneself—literally find oneself—engaged in one or another of the goofy conversations that would be ensuing in every corner of the house, as did Gurney and I the night we determined that behind the peg-board on Chloe's kitchen wall lurked an enormous baby chick, ready to pounce on us, bellowing, in a voice like Bullmoose Jackson's, "PEEP! PEEP!" Or somebody might cut open an old golf ball and start unwinding the endless rubber band inside, and in moments a roomful of merrymakers would be hopelessly ensnarled in a rubbery web, writhing hilariously—a surreal tableau which, to my peyote-enchanted eyes, was astonishingly beautiful, and was entitled *We're All in This Thing Together.*

At one party, Gurney maneuvered ten delirious revelers into the back yard, looped Chloe's fifty-foot clothesline about them, and endeavored to create the World's Largest Cat's Cradle. "Awright now, men," he kept bawling at his troops, "I want all the thumbs to raise their hands!"

Well, okay, you had to be there. No denying there was plenty of unmitigated adolescent silliness in all those hijinks—just as there's no denying the unfortunate similarity between my experience at *West Side Story* and that of the celebrated Little Moron, the one who beats himself on the head with a hammer because it feels so good to stop. But like the man in the aftershave commercial, we *needed* that, some of us, to wake us from the torpor of the fifties. To be sure, there were casualties—those who couldn't put the hammer down till they'd pounded their poor heads to jelly, those who blissed out or blasted off, those for whom dope was a purgative and every trip a bad trip, an exorcism. And I'm also perfectly willing to concede, if I must, that there were just as many others who successfully expanded their consciousnesses to wonderful dimensions through the miracle of chemistry.

But for weekenders and day-trippers like me, psychedelics were mostly just for laughs; they made things more funny-ha-ha than funny-peculiar. And for me at least, the laughter was a value in itself. I hadn't laughed so unrestrainedly since childhood, and the effect was refreshing, bracing, invigorating —aftershave for the psyche. Nor had I ever in my life allowed myself to fall so utterly in love with all my friends at once. And there were several occasions, in the highest, clearest moments of those high old times, when I caught a glimpse of something at the periphery of my vision that shook the throne of the tyrannical little atheist who sat in my head and ruled my Kentucky Methodist heart.

It was all too good to last, of course. Quick as the wink of a strobe light, Kennedy had fallen to Lee Harvey Oswald, the Vietnam issue was as hot as a two-dollar pistol, the country was a-boil with racial unrest . . . and Perry Lane had gone under to the developers. The times, they were a-changin', and not for the better, either. The first day of the rest of our lives was over.

THREE

A Misdemeanor Against Nature

.

A man should be jailed for
telling lies to the young.

—LILLIAN HELLMAN

AUGUST 1968, the very week of the Democratic
Party's unhappy soiree in Chicago, and all across
the linth and breadth of this gret land (as the poli-
ticians on TV had been bleating all week long)
there hung a sulphurous cloud of suspicion and
malevolence as foully palpable as smog, and there
I was in what had to be among the worst places in
the continental U.S. for a man of my political and
social inclinations at the time, just pulling into the
parking lot of the Penington Club tavern on Highway 52 in Aberdeen, Ohio.

This stretch of Highway 52 winds along the north
bank of the Ohio River for about twenty miles,
from Ripley through Aberdeen to Manchester, and
there was a time in my life when I knew it as well
as I know the way to my own bathroom. At Aberdeen, there's a toll-free bridge across the Ohio to
Maysville, Kentucky, the hometown of my high
school and college years . . . and since Ohio per-
mits the sale of 3.2 beer to eighteen-year-olds,
whereas in Maysville you can't darken a tavern door
until you're twenty-one—and then only until ten
o'clock at night—that bridge loomed as large as the
Golden Gate in the landscape of my adolescence.

For the Buckeye he is a crafty breed, and in the
days of my youth, Highway 52 was fairly lined with
taverns—the Top Hat and the Terrace Club and

the Bay Horse and the Penington Club and a dozen others—rank, musty, low-ceilinged places with puke in the urinals and Cowboy Copas on the jukebox and lighting feeble enough to allow a fifteen-year-old to pass for eighteen if the bartender wasn't in a mood to split hairs, which he hardly ever was. Some of those havens have long since yielded to mom-and-pop motels and Col. Seersucker's Kentucky Possum Tartare stands, but in 1968 a remarkable number of them were still unscathed by progress. And the unscathiest of all was the scrofulous old Penington Club, where even then I had already been wasting my substance in riotous living off and on for almost twenty years.

To which purpose I found myself that August night, as I did every summer when I came home to Kentucky for a visit, about to sally into the Penington Club once more. Ordinarily a happy moment for me, this, a moment filled almost to bursting with anticipation; nostalgic nitwit that I am, I can be moved to the point of tears by the raunchy familiarity of such places, the sweet memories of revels best forgotten.

By 1968, you may as well know, I had become a to-the-manner-born New Age Californian, with all the rights, privileges, and irresponsibilities that are the natural birthright of that favored race. I had also become, improbably enough, a bona fide member of the faculty of Stanford University, my Wallace E. Stegner Fellowship having miraculously transmogri-

fied itself into an Edward H. Jones Visiting Lecture-
ship way back in 1963.

Clearly, though, I was no visitor. I was more like
the Man Who Came to Dinner; they couldn't have
run me out of California with a stick. Since 1966
I'd lived, with my first wife, Kit, and our burgeoning
family, in a big old house in downtown Palo Alto
that had become a sort of Southern way station for
Bay Area freakdom. Kesey and his troupe, the
Pranksters, were in and out all the time, as was a
steady parade of peace activists, revolutionaries,
Whole Earth Catalog visionaries, associate professors of touchy-feely from the Free University, Black
Panthers, White Panthers, Gray Panthers, Red
Guards (they lacked the sense of humor to call themselves Pink Panthers, so I'll do it for them), dealers
and dopers and Diggers, gurus and swamis and
Sufis, psychodrama honchos, Hairless Krishnas, the
occasional Hell's Angel . . . and, once, the FBI. It
was like living in the national center of gravity, or
in one of those ubiquitous California tourist traps
called Mystery Spots, places where gravitational
and magnetic forces are supposedly concentrated in
such a way as to inspire water to flow upstream,
marbles to roll up inclines, birds to fall from the sky
like rocks. I pretended I was working on my novel—
but you can't write a novel in a place like that; the
words just won't stay on the page.

Naturally, my enthusiasms had continued to mani-
fest themselves in the form of certain subtle changes

in my outward aspect: As I pulled into the Penington
Club parking lot that night, I was wearing high-
heeled, pointy-toed, zip-up frootboots and tie-dyed
bells and an over-the-collar mod-bob and a Genghis
Khan mustache and round, mellow-yellow granny
glasses—a set of accessories not likely to take the
best-dressed barfly award in Penington's, where the
clientele's taste ran at its very dandiest to bowling
shirts and engineer boots, and not the first sign of
a facial hair below the eyebrows. Already my little
affectations, modest as they'd seemed at home in
Palo Alto, had won me wide-eyed stares on the
streets of Maysville. It was the specs, I think, that
did it, those piss-muckledy-dun Ben Franklins which,
representing as they did a fairly substantial commitment of cold cash, seemed to confirm what my
other trappings strongly hinted at: *It's a hippie it's
a yippie it's a Commie it's a California crazy it's a
fruit-cup it's a freak!* Not exactly the sort of recep-
tion a sensible and prudent thirty-six-year-old peda-
gogue and father of three would ordinarily choose
to be accorded by the usual Friday-night crowd in
Penington's—farmhands and construction workers
and beer-truck drivers on a busman's holiday, any
number of whom would no doubt just as leave knock
me on my California ass as look at me. Indeed, would
very much rather.

And as a matter of convenient fact, it just so
happened that I had my regular old black horn-rims
right in the glove compartment; put them there
myself, if you must know, against just such a con-

tingency as this. But were there not matters of principle involved here? Had I not the inalienable right—the duty, even!—to go about looking like a perfect simpleton if I chose? And hadn't I always prided myself on my success at turning my conservative Stanford colleagues' hostility into curiosity into what passed, at faculty cocktail parties, for communication? And although I'm probably the most inept bar fighter since Ethelred the Unready, was I not big enough to *look* fairly formidable to a not-too-discerning eye?

Unto the breach, then. In a matter of moments I was sitting at the Penington Club bar with a beer in front of me, sitting there in the neon smaze and the blare of shouted conversation and beery laughter and Red Sovine mourning "Little Rosa" at the top of the Wurlitzer's electronic lungs, and so far not a soul had uttered an unkind word, or even looked too very askance at me. So it was just paranoia after all, I scolded myself, just hippie-dippy paranoia compounded by my own unseemly willingness to think the worst of my countrymen. Clearly I owed them an apology, perhaps a musical salute to demonstrate that, despite my alien getup and my California appetites and my *à la mode* politics, I stood foursquare with them against the barbarian hordes. Taking my beer along, I left my barstool and ambled over to the jukebox, plugged it with a couple of quarters, and picked myself a nice bouquet of country songs. Then I made my way between the tables to a booth over against the wall, where I settled down to drink my beer and listen to Patsy Cline sing "I'll Sail My Ship Alone" and watch a two-hundred-pound lady and her one-hundred-pound gentleman friend play shuffleboard.

But no sooner had I set my leaky rowboat of a mind adrift with Patsy's ship in these familiar and relatively tranquil waters than I became aware of some sort of minor turbulence at my shoulder, a gentle but insistent jostling, and I looked up to find a large, lubberly young Penington Clubber towering over me, shaking my shoulder with a heavy hand and grinning down at me in a way that did little to enhance my peace of mind. Instinctively, I glanced toward the door. ("Whenever they get his chicken-shit up," a college drinking buddy used to sing of me, to the tune of "Clancy Lowered the Boom," "McClanahan leaves the room-room-room.") But this crew-cut young stalwart had had the foresight to position himself between me and the exit, so strategic withdrawal was not among my options. Essaying a friendly—not to say craven—little grin of my own, I looked up at him inquiringly and squeaked some idiotic greeting.

"Hey there, Hairy," he said, almost—but not quite—affably, "you're kinda hairy, ain't you?"

The question seemed pretty strictly rhetorical, so I ventured a hangdog "Who, me?" gesture and, in the wisdom of my years, kept my big California mouth shut.

"You see that guy over there?" He pointed to a

nearby table, where, in fact, two guys sat watching us. But there wasn't the least doubt which of the two he had in mind. The big scrapper. The big, thick-necked, dark-haired lout of a youth who was even at that very moment favoring me with an indolent, almost pitying smile. His smaller companion, who was crumbling oyster crackers into a bowl of bean soup, eyed me as though I were a foreign body that had turned up in his soup spoon.

"I mean that black-headed one," the crew-cut explained unnecessarily. "You know what he called you, Hairy? He called you a fucken punk."

Well, here it is, hot shot, I told myself. Your big moment, your chance to become the youngest old crock in history to cross the Generation Gap on a tightrope . . . backward.

"No, wait now," my interlocutor ponderously corrected himself, "I got that wrong. He never said you was a fucken punk, he just said you was a punk. *I* was the one that said you was a fucken punk."

He turned to the other table. "Hey, Estill!" he called above the din. Estill rose and shambled toward us, growing taller and broader by the step. He was carrying his empty beer bottle by the neck. A bad sign.

"Hey, Estill," the crew-cut said, "I was just tellin' old Hairy here that we called him a fucken punk."

Estill flipped me a diffident little two-fingered salute with the hand that wasn't holding the beer bottle. "Naw, Parky," he said, "now you know we never said he was a fucken punk. All we said was, he *looks* like a fucken punk."

"Well," I offered hopefully, "I guess you all are entitled to your own opinion."

Estill heartily concurred in my championing of the fine old principles of democratic egalitarianism. "You better believe it," he said. "And my opinion is, if you ain't a fucken punk, you woulda done got up and kicked the livin' shit out of us."

"Whaddya say, Hairy?" Parky chortled. "Has Estill got your number?"

"I'll tell you what," I said, begging the question. "How about if you all sit down and let me buy you a beer instead. Maybe we'll get along better than we think."

Speak swiftly, Kesey used to say, and carry a big soft.

Suddenly a lot was riding on what happened next. Because wasn't this exactly what the Richie Rich revolutionaries at Stanford were forever exhorting us to do, to take our ideals out among the People, and Make the Revolution? And there was also the sobering fact that if somebody did get the livin' shit kicked out of him, I could be reasonably sure it wouldn't be Estill or Parky.

Those stout defenders of the status quo, meanwhile, were exchanging smirks, as if to say, Well, if the fucken punk wants to buy us a beer before we kick the livin' shit out of him . . . Then Estill slid into the other side of the booth, and Parky, following his lead, dropped into the seat beside me. Breathing a little easier, I signaled anxiously to the barmaid, who'd been keeping a watchful eye on the proceedings, for three more beers.

"Listen," I began, fumbling for the beer money, "in the first place, I'm too damned old to fight with you guys, if I can get out of it. I'll bet I'm half again as old as either one of you all."

It was not, let me hasten to explain, that I imagined I looked notably younger than my years; just that I suspected Estill and Parky hadn't yet seen through my flower-child getup to the doddering old trentagenarian behind it. And they were still young enough themselves that they might be impressed by my seniority.

"Shit you are," Estill said. On the TV screen behind the bar, a space-helmeted Chicago policeman was beating some poor long-hair senseless with his nightstick.

"Well, I'm thirty-six. I graduated from Maysville High School in 1951. That's over seventeen years ago."

"Shit you did," said Parky. "You mean to tell me you're from Maysville?"

"I sure am. I grew up in Brooksville, over in Bracken County. But I went to Maysville High for three years."

"Wait a damn minute," Estill said. "I've lived around here a long time, bud, and I never seen nothing looks like you in Maysville." He said "you" as if it tasted bad.

"I don't live here anymore," I told him. "I live in California now."

"California!" Parky marveled. "Sure enough?"

Far out, as we Californians say; Parky was already coming around. But Estill would be another matter.

"California?" he pressed me. "What do you do in California?"

"I'm a schoolteacher. I teach English."

"Shit you do. You ain't no damn schoolteacher, lookin' like that."

"Well," I said, "they don't pay as much attention to that kind of thing in California, I guess."

"Must not," Estill sneered. "What grade do you teach?"

"I teach in college, actually."

"He could be tellin' the truth there, Estill," Parky said. "When I went down to Briarhopper State that semester, they had some English teachers down there that was queer as three-dollar bills."

"They might have some of those where I teach, too," I had to allow, "but I'm not one of them. I'm a married man, myself. In fact, I've got three kids."

"They tell me some of your biggest queers is married men," Estill grumbled. "Hey, Rick," he called across the room to their companion, who was polishing off his bean soup at the other table, "this guy says he went to Maysville High."

"He shit, too," Rick demurred. He got up and

stalked over to our booth, bug-looking me all the way, and sat down next to Estill. "When were you ever at Maysville High?" he demanded, glaring across the table at me as if the very suggestion amounted to a desecration of the Temple of Learning.

I went there three years, I told him; I graduated in '51.

"You shit, too. Because listen here, I went to Maysville High School all my life, by God, and my whole damn *family* went to Maysville High School, and my brother Jerry, by God, *he* graduated in '51! So don't you tell *me*, by God, that you . . ."

"You're Jerry O'Dell's little brother! You're Rickie-O! Hey, I went to *school* with Jerry!"

Saved! Singled out by Fate's fickle digit, that I might live to revolute again! Little Rickie-O, whose brother Jerry-O had been one of my favorite co-pilots when we'd cruised the midnight streets of Maysville in my fabled Chevy Bel Air! Old Digger O'Dell! Why, we'd logged more flight time together than Van Johnson and Dana Andrews! And here was little Rickie-O!

But in my delight at this unexpected turn of events, I'd momentarily forgotten that Rickie-O still didn't know who *I* was. In fact, he was at that very moment leaning across the table peering intently at me, without the slightest flicker of recognition. Seventeen years is a long time; what if he didn't remember me?

"My name's Ed McClanahan," I prompted, searching his face for some reaction. For the first few seconds, nothing. Then, spurred by sudden inspiration, I took off my glasses; and as I lowered them, Rickie-O straightened slowly, raised his eyes to the cobweb-festooned ceiling, and dramatically clapped a palm to his forehead.

"Eddie McClanahan!" he cried. "Why, you stupid sons-of-bitches, this guy went to school with Jerry! Why, this here was one of the smartest guys in Maysville High School! Why, this guy teaches college somewheres, ain't that right, Eddie? Why, this goddamned hippie is twice as old and twice as smart as both of you two half-asses put together, and you all wantin' to punch him out!"

Then Rickie-O was pumping my hand energetically, and we were both grinning and giggling, and Estill was hiding his face behind his hands in mock humiliation. "Hey, Park," he said, "you know what you are, don't you?"

"Yeah, Estill," Parky snickered. "I'm a fucken punk."

Well, it was the beginning of a brief but otherwise perfect friendship. I spent the next couple of hours in the Penington Club drinking beer with Estill and Parky and Rickie-O, and the next couple of hours after that drinking coffee with them at the truck stop down the road. And while we were together I told them all I knew—and a good deal more besides —about the vital social issues of the day, about peace and love and civil rights and cops and dope and hippies and yippies and swingers and nude beaches and topless shoeshine parlors, and by the time we parted company they'd learned more about some of those matters, perhaps, than was good for them. As I drove home, giddy in the dawn, I congratulated myself happily for having finally pitched in and propagated the counterculture on my home turf, and lived to tell the tale. Mess with an English teacher, would they! Up the revolution!

I wish I could also testify now that, in my hour of triumph, I'd remembered to toss a few crumbs of credit to Estill and Parky and Rickie-O, who'd had the good grace to spare a Perfect Simpleton his comeuppance, and the good manners to listen politely to his heresies—and possibly even to have taken a few of them to heart. But I'm afraid that when it came to credit, I gathered most of it unto myself.

And not until years and years later, when I too had become a Kentuckian again, did it come to me that in the Penington Club that night, in my own small and, I trust, ineffectual way, I had aided and abetted a ravishing of innocence: the Californication of Kentucky.

FOUR

Rouse Up, O Young Men of the New Age!

IN the latter 1960s, on a corner in downtown Palo Alto scarcely a brickbat's throw from the Stanford campus, there stood an aged, derelict, three-story brick office building, the first floor of which was occupied by a fish 'n' chips 'n' rock 'n' roll establishment called the Poppycock. Upstairs, the sweaty-hatband gents who managed the building had rented out the old offices, formerly the domain of perfectly respectable doctors, realtors, and accounting firms, to an assortment of artists, writers, sex therapists, filmmakers, and anarcho-syndicalist organizations dedicated to the violent overthrow of whatever wasn't nailed down.

And I was a primary ingredient of this unsavory mélange, having rented, on the very day the sweaty hatbands took over in 1967, for the speaks-for-itself sum of twenty-five dollars a month, the second-floor office directly above the Poppycock's bandstand. In this grimy, scrod-scented aerie, with the jackhammer syncopations of Big Brother and the Holding Company or the early Grateful Dead rattling the floorboards at my feet, I composed my rhapsodic odes to the revolutionary spirit of the times, for publication in *The Free You*, of which I was a fearless editor.

Beneath my window, meanwhile, the beat went

on day and night; the sidewalks swarmed with rock 'n' roll riffraff, adolescent acidheads and swiftly aging speedsters, motorcycle madmen and wilted flower children, slightly unhinged outpatients from the nearby VA hospital, spare-changers and affluent musicians and plainclothesmen and nouveau riche dealers, all the myriad varieties of California white trash. Street-corner preachers and peace-movement pitchmen harangued the passersby; in the shadows, furtive retail and wholesale transactions were negotiated by shifty-eyed entrepreneurs and consumers. Now and then, there was a peace march on University Avenue; once, a riot. The Poppycock corner was where It was indisputably At in Palo Alto. If ever an old would-Beat had found his little piece of heaven, I'd found mine.

Nonetheless, late in the fall of '68, when with the chilly weather the street people began to invade the upstairs of the building, prowling the dim, scabrous hallways like vermin in the hide of some mangy old mutt, holding court in the unoccupied offices, performing their unholy rituals in the toilets, the mellow vibes started to ring a little sour. One November night in the darkened hall, I stumbled over an astonishingly pungent wino, who roused himself just long enough to announce that he was the new night watchman, before he crashed again. Another time, someone stole the padlock right off my office door while I was inside working. Several times my doorway was employed as a *pissoir*. Finally, in December, someone jimmied my new padlock and made off with an antiquated thesaurus and a packet of Pearly Gates morning-glory seeds.

All of which is why, late one night during the Christmas holidays, I went out of my way to swing by the Poppycock and check out my office as I drove home after a party. The weather had turned decidedly nippy during the past few days, and as a consequence the traffic in the halls had been especially heavy; only that afternoon I'd been interrupted at my inflammatory scribblings by a door-to-door acid salesman, then by a pair of giggling fourteen-year-old androgynes who were *buying* acid door-to-door, and finally by the aromatic night watchman, who put the arm on me for fifty cents as a reward for keeping such a sharp eye on things. So I was apprehensive.

Sure enough, I'd had more callers. This time they'd busted the door clear off its hinges and appropriated my radio and my brand-new, nifty little hundred-dollar Hermes portable typewriter, which at the time I treasured above all things except, possibly, my mustache. The radio was an elderly, malfunctioning table model with an intolerable frog in its throat; if the counterculture was that hard up for a radio, I wouldn't begrudge it. But the typewriter was an altogether other matter. Why, stealing the tools of a writer's trade is a counter-revolutionary act, it's positively reactionary, a crime against humanity itself! And to add insult to injury, the barbarians had strewn my manuscripts and papers about the premises in a manner suggesting a profound disrespect for Art. So I did what any reasonable, responsible apostate would do under the circumstances: I called the cops.

They came immediately, two grave, businesslike young patrolmen who strode in right past the spray-painted OFF THE PIGS! legends with which one of the building's unofficial tenants had thoughtfully decorated the hallways, strode into my office and looked around, and strode right back out again. Nothing they could do, they said, unless I had the serial number of the typewriter and it happened to turn up in a pawnshop. But surely there was *something*, I fumed. How about fingerprints? Nope, the patrolmen said, not a chance—for hadn't I myself already poked about the room in search of clues like Dick Tracy's inept rookie in "The Crimestopper's Textbook," smudging fingerprints wherever I touched?

"I tell you what, Mr. Lannieham," mused one of the cops on his way out, "if I was writing *me* a book in this place, I believe I'd use a pencil."

So, finally, deep in the middle of the night, I battened down the hatches as best I could and grumbled my way home to bed, where I fell into an uneasy sleep and dreamed grumpy cartoon dreams in which my lovely little Hermes sprouted wings and blithely flew away, as I groaned into my pillow. In the morning, rather earlier than I might have chosen, I was awakened by . . .

* * *

. . . the phone. "Ed?" a dimly familiar voice inquires, rather tentatively. "This is Whitey." A pause, while I ruminate on that. Then: "You know. Whitey? That used to be in your writing class?"

"Um, um, oh yeah. Whitey. Right, right." And slowly a face emerges out of the recent past: Whitey, a Stanford grad student in another department, who'd taken my creative-writing course last spring; a long-haired, semi-serious radical from Texas, a little older than most of my students, and a pretty fair country writer when it came to that. "How you making it, Whitey? What's new?" I am polite but wary; I can feel a request for a letter of recommendation coming on, and I'm not in a real accommodating frame of mind just now. If Whitey wants me to write a recommendation for him, I'll tell him I can't because some damn long-haired Commie hippie ding-dong stole my damn typewriter, that's what I'll tell him.

But Whitey graciously overlooks my lack of warmth. "Listen, Ed," he is already saying, "lemme ask you a question, and if the answer's no, then just forget I asked it, okay?"

Uh-oh, sounds like the old letter-of-recommendation song and dance, all right. "Yeah, sure," I tell him, barely suppressing a grouchy sigh. "Go ahead, I guess."

"Well then, tell me: did you get ripped off last night?"

Say what? Suddenly I am sitting bolt upright in

bed, with my ear socked like a suction cup to the receiver. "Yeah, I did, I sure did!"

"A typewriter and a radio, maybe?"

"Yeah, right!"

"Well, listen"—Whitey is speaking almost in whispers now, and hastily—"listen, if you can come over to my place right away, I think I can get it back for you, the typewriter anyhow. The guys that took it are friends of this chick I live with, see, and they came by and tried to sell it to me. When I found out they ripped it off from upstairs in the Poppy-cock, I sort of thought it might be yours. One of them is still here, and I think he'll give it back, if you ask him for it. You better hurry, though. I don't know how long I can keep him here."

Hey hey, a freaking miracle! I nearly garrote my-self with the phone cord getting together a pencil and paper to take down Whitey's address, and within minutes I have scooped up my writer friend Wig, who's visiting from back East and has evinced an unwholesome desire to experience the California Thing to the fullest, and we are zipping across town in my—you guessed it—VW Microbus, the McClana-van, and I am blithering merrily away about how this is, after all, the Christmas season, and I am, after all, a generous, large-spirited sort who'll prob-ably let bygones be bygones as long as I get my type-writer back, blah-blah-blah. It will be a while yet before it occurs to me that such generosity as has been displayed so far has been entirely on the part of Whitey, and of the thief himself. By the time we reach Whitey's east Palo Alto neighborhood—a semi-genteel ghetto shared by working-class blacks and white Stanford students—I have once again persuaded myself that I am the hero of my own life story.

As we curb the McClanavan before a shabby old gray stucco house with the windowshades all pulled, so that it looks out upon the world with a blank, noncommittal stare, I note that squarely in the middle of the tiny, blighted front yard there stands, for all the world like one of those little cast-iron jockeys that grace the front yards of Southern manses, a middle-aged gentleman of color, regarding us with baleful eye from beneath the bill of an improbably spiffy-looking golf cap. Could this be our man? Suddenly it occurs to me that I may be dealing here not with some trifling amateur but with genuine, grown-up criminals, second-story men, hardened Hermes-nappers. Black Panthers, even. If they demand a ransom, how high can I go before I meet my lofty revolutionary principles coming down?

"Yawl huntin' Whitey?" this striking fixture demands as I alight before him. And when, quailing inwardly, I confirm our mission with a nod, it is as if I have popped the cork on a Neal Cassady genie, another Talking Dervish.

"Me too!" he cries, hurrying to join us at Whitey's doorstep. "Me too, I was jis goin' to see ole Whitey my*seff*, I was down at the A & *Pee* sto' this mornin', see, and that sto' guy, he say, Jabbers, yawl want this here trash, I gone th'ow hit out if you don't want hit? And dog if he don't gimme a whole gret big ole *bag* of rotten p'*taters*, and t'*maters*, and *squarsh* and all, you never see the like, *vedgibles* y'see. So I taken hit home wimme, and my ole woman she say, Jabbers, you blame ole fool you, I ain't eatin' no sich damn ole rubbage as that, hee hee hee; she say you gwan crost the street to that ole hippie's house and axe him does *he* want this ole stuff. So I'm gonna axe ole Whitey could he use 'em, they jis what he *need* y'see, ole skinny long-hair thing, he make him some good vedgible *soup* y'see . . ."

Jabbers indeed. It is the first wash of a floodtide of words that seems to flow from him ceaselessly and effortlessly, an aimless torrent that begins nowhere and goes nowhere and ends nowhere, as if his tongue has somehow come unfastened at both ends and blithers on of its own free will and accord, cut loose from its last flimsy moorings to his mind. Right away I detect the breath of Sneaky Pete upon the air, and I understand that this here is no doped-up desperado, no cat burglar, no fiery black Maoist bent upon the radical restructuring of the social order by appropriating the equipment of capitalist-road writers. This here is the neighborhood lush, is who this is; Uncle Remus's long-lost no-'count nephew.

Now Jabbers is rapping briskly at the door, still talking like a teapot: "That Whitey, he all *right*, by God, he tole me he *fo'* the black man, he even got him a big ole pitcher of a Nee-grow right on his wall in there, one of these Black Pampher boogers holdin' him a big ole *gun*, look mean as *hell*, by God!

So I gonna give ole Whitey all the rotten vedgibles he can *eat*, y'see, cause he good to Jabbers, him and that Miss Mercy, that li'l girly of his'n, she gimme a li'l taste of po't *wine* one time, so I . . ."

The door opens, and Whitey is standing in the hallway, looking pretty much the same as when I'd last seen him, back in the early autumn. He's got a little more hair, I suppose, but then for that matter so do I. Who, in fact, does not, these days?

"Hey, come in," he says amiably. "Where'd you find old Jabbers?"

He does not wait for an answer, giving Wig and me to understand that we might have found Jabbers almost anywhere. Whitey is friendly, but as we enter I notice that he keeps peering anxiously over my shoulder to the street, as though he is expecting someone to slip in behind us. Later I am to discover that his anxiety has to do with some utterly unrelated negotiations he has going with yet another set of people, who are due to arrive momentarily—but just now I have no way of knowing that, so Whitey's uneasiness is making me uneasy too. As he leads us down the darkened hall toward the kitchen, I feel as jittery as an overwound windup toy; at any moment I might disintegrate in a small explosion of tiny springs and cogwheels.

". . . got t'maters over there *this* big, by God; some of 'em ain't got no rotten places a-*tall*, hardly. Yawl wouldn' have a li'l taste of sweet po't *wine* fo' ole Jabbers, I don't reckon? I sho' could use me a . . ."

Then we are in the kitchen, and there, sitting at a table piled high with dirty dishes, pots and pans, old newspapers, books, manuscripts—in short, the kind of kitchen table no self-respecting graduate student would be without—sitting there at one end of the table is a very pretty girl—Miss Mercy? Was that what Jabbers called her?—with a blond baby on her lap, and across from her sits what has to be the scruffiest hippie west of Marrakesh. I recognize him right off. He's a Poppycock regular, just a kid, maybe seventeen or eighteen, a barefoot psychedelic waif with a pale, pinched, meager little face beneath a wild snarl of dark, matted hair that reaches half-way down his back, and a wispy little-boy goatee, and a meticulously filthy old plaid flannel shirt with the sleeves half rotted away, and about a dozen greasy leather pouches, stuffed with who-knows-what insalubrious substances, dangling from the belt loops of his crusty jeans. As we file into the room Whitey says to him, "This is Ed," and through the hanging veil of hair he looks up at me, me and my eighteen-dollar Mod Squad coif and my eighty-dollar granny glasses, looks up at me with the sweetest, saddest, shyest, most winning smile, an exquisitely lovely *gift* of a smile, and holds out his hand for me to shake, and says, softly and with perfect ingenuousness:

"Hey, man, meet the cat that ripped off your type-writer!"

"That's Yogurt," Whitey says. "I already told him you were coming."

Then we, Yogurt and I, are shaking hands and giggling and clapping each other on the back like long-lost Oddfellows, and I am charmed beyond measure, and utterly won over.

". . . I b'lieve I better give ole Yogurt some good rotten t'maters *too*, look to me like he need somethin' to clean hisself out, them t'maters be jis the trick . . ."

I am beginning to realize that Jabbers's gibberish is to social intercourse what the tamboura is to Indian music, a kind of liquid atonal drone that rushes along just beneath the surface of the conversation, bubbling up like a wellspring whenever there's the smallest silence.

"Listen, man," Yogurt is imploring me, "I mean, I got to tell you, man, like, we wouldn't *never*'ve ripped off your shit if we would've known you were a hip dude!"

Me? A hip dude? Me, this aging Peter Pan in pointy boots? Surely he can't mean it, surely he's setting me up for some awful put-down. But his voice and hangdog expression are so freighted with earnest apology that finally I'm unable to harbor the slightest doubt of his sincerity. It is perhaps the grandest compliment I've been paid in my whole life . . . so grand that it completely crowds out of my consciousness the fact that, however much it distresses him to have to confess to having ripped off a hip dude, Yogurt is not the least bit abashed at admitting he's a thief.

"Oh, that's all right," I hear myself reassure him,

half apologetically. "In fact, I don't really care at all about the radio, you all can keep that if you want to. I would kind of like to have the typewriter back, though, if you could see your way clear to . . ."

"Hey, no problem, man!" Yogurt reassures *me*. "It's cool, it's cool! The only thing is, I ain't got it with me right now. Who's got it right now is Wheatgerm and the Beast."

Wheatgerm? The Beast? Uh oh.

". . . now, you gonna make you some mash p'taters, you jis mash up them little rotten parts right in, you won't never hardly know they in there . . ."

"Yeah, Wheatgerm and the Beast took it all with them, see. But I'll go find them, man, and score it back for you! Hey, man, I'll go right now, yeah, hey!" In a sudden burst of zeal he leaps up from the table, and I see all over again how pitifully frail he is. A rag, a bone, a hank of hair, that's Yogurt. "Hey, why don't *everybody* come, shit yeah, let's go find this dude's shit for him!"

Almost at once he has the whole roomful of people —remember now, there's Whitey and the girl and the baby and Jabbers (". . . I bet ole Beast'd *love* to have some nice squarsh . . .") and Wig and me and, oh yeah, Yogurt's big black dog, who as I recall was under the table until Yogurt stood up and brought the dog up with him, like some kind of strangely malformed shadow—all of us suddenly swirling about this cramped little kitchen in the wake of Yogurt's enthusiasm, which is already propelling Yogurt himself out of the kitchen and down the hall toward the front door. And now somehow the entire mass has packed itself like a school of compliant sardines into a space about one-third as large as the kitchen we've just escaped, and Jabbers is babbling and Yogurt is inviting us to go with him and we are declining and the baby is babbling hardly less coherently than Jabbers, and the dog—whose neck, it develops, is bound by a length of twine to Yogurt's wrist—is barking gaily; and then there is a knock at the door and Whitey opens it and admits two guys who are obviously the ones he has been expecting, two long-haired, beady-eyed types with their collars turned up and their hands jammed into their coat pockets, one of them with a package under his arm that doubtless contains a variety of vedgible matter that Whitey really has been pining for.

Whitey coughs nervously and asks the newcomers if they've come to look at the room, heh heh, and they cough nervously and say, Oh yeah, the room, heh heh, and Whitey shuffles his feet anxiously, making ready to lead them off, but before they can get mobilized, Yogurt parts the assembled multitudes by leaping to the little peephole window in the door, and peers out and giggles and announces, "Uh oh, this is gonna get interestin'! Here comes Wheatgerm and the Beast!"

The door swings open and somebody yells, Hey, Wheatgerm! and in bops a Chaplinesque little bundle of rags and bone and hair who could be Yogurt's double and is, in fact (someone tells me later), his first cousin. The two of them fling themselves into each other's arms, embracing and crying out each other's name—"Yogurt baby!" "Wheatgerm!"—as joyously as if they haven't crossed paths in years and years; and I relax a little, thinking, If this is the biggest size they come in, I guess I'll be okay.

Until the door swings open one more time, and into the melee strides a great, slab-shouldered, scowling ogre wearing biker's leathers and cycle boots and a thick chain for a belt, and the most remarkable head of hair I've ever seen, a dense yellow shock the shape and color and texture of a haystack, with a short, ropy queue that swings loose from the crown of his skull; and within this strange hummock of hair are these pale, cold, blue eyes glowering, darting furiously from face to face in the sullen half-light of the hallway. A griffin with a lion's mane and the fierce eye of an eagle; a very Caliban. Behold, the Beast!

And the dog is yipping and Jabbers is yapping and the baby is yowling and Yogurt and Wheatgerm are whooping and Whitey and his colleagues are mumbling conspiratorially behind their hands, and we are all milling around, treading on one another's feet—all of us, that is, except the Beast, who stands motionless and silent in the midst of all this clamor, savagely glaring straight at me.

But before I can give more than passing consideration to Wig's and my chances if we were to bolt for the door, Yogurt wraps one arm around

Wheatgerm's shoulders and the other around the
Beast's waist and draws them through the burgeoning assemblage to where I'm standing and cries
above the din:

"Hey, you guys, meet the cat that we ripped the
typewriter off of!"

". . . or you could squeeze you some of them
t'maters and make you some nice *jewce*, which that
reminds me, I don't reckon you all would have a li'l
sip or two of . . ."

The Beast is squinting into the gloom, his ice-blue
eyes just inches from my own, his small mouth
working slowly, as if he savors the taste of the rage
that's rising in his gorge. Our eyes stay locked that
way until, after the longest possible time, he reaches
out and grabs my hand and pumps it vigorously,
exclaiming:

"Aw, no shit, man, was that your place? Hey,
listen, man, we wouldn't *never*'ve ripped you off if
we knew you was a hip dude!"

"Right, man!" Wheatgerm concurs enthusiastically, pumping my other hand and breaking into an
ecstatic little dance of mock dismay. "Right, we
wouldn't *never* rip off a hip dude!"

"We gotta get this dude's shit, man!" cries
Yogurt. "Where's it at, man?"

"The typewriter's over at the other place, man,"
Wheatgerm offers.

"Yeah," the Beast says, turning back to me. "We
can get the typewriter right now, man, no sweat.

It's over at this place where we slept at last night. But listen, man, I ain't so sure about your radio. Because the thing is, see, the Spirit's got that."

The Spirit?

". . . I tell yawl what, I jis let yawl have that whole big ole *bag* of truck, if somebody jis gimme *one li'l ole half pint* of . . ."

"Right!" Yogurt pipes. "Let's go get the dude's typewriter, before the Spirit gets it! This here's a good dude, man, let's go get his shit for him!"

"Yeah!" Wheatgerm chimes in, and "Shit yes!" bellows the Beast, and the dog yelps something that sounds a lot like "Fucking-A!" And Yogurt flings open the door, and to my astonishment the four of them split, vanish, evaporate before my very eyes!

Watching the door swing shut behind them, I am once again beset by doubts. Have I stood here and watched my three yeggs stroll out the door scot-free and never fired a shot? Has my Hermes really spread its little wings and flown the coop for good?

Meanwhile, the congestion in the hall is easing as quickly as it had set in. Whitey waves me an indifferent farewell, and he and his misanthropic associates, still growling among themselves, slouch off toward the rear of the house (that will be the last we'll see of them, by the way; they never reappeared while Wig and I were there), and the baby toddles through a doorway off the hall, and Jabbers toddles after him (". . . you wait up there, li'l buddy, ole Uncle Jabbers gonna git you some nice squarsh . . ."), and the girl follows them and Wig

follows her and I follow Wig. We find ourselves in
the living room, which is pretty thoroughly littered
with the baby's toys, but otherwise rather barren,
except for a couple of worn, overstuffed chairs and
a rump-sprung couch, beneath which skulks what at
first appears to be some species of rodent, but soon
turns out instead to be a very small Chihuahua, hairless as a jalapeño, and not a great deal larger.

"Come on out, Thor," the girl languidly summons
this uncomely quadruped, as she gathers up the baby
and settles herself on the couch. "That big old
doggy's all gone now. But don't you worry, man,"
she adds, turning to me, "they'll be right back, I
betcha. They'll bring back your typer thingy too,
you see if they don't."

Thor, after assuring himself that the coast is
really clear, creeps out from under the couch and
prances like a rat on stilts across the floor to Wig's
chair, where he throws himself upon Wig's ankle
and begins making ardent love to his desert boot.

I slump wearily onto the couch beside the girl.
"Sure," I am halfheartedly declaring, "I believe it,
I know they will."

Wig, to the vast amusement of Jabbers, is striving
desperately to scrape the amorous Thor off his foot
on the leg of his chair. "Hee hee!" Jabbers exults.
"I jis wisht you'd looky here at ole Thor humpin'
on this ball-headed boy!"

The girl has heard the way my voice sagged beneath the weight of disbelief. "*Truly* they will, man,"
she assures me serenely. "They're beautiful dudes!"

I try to say "They are!" But despite my best effort it comes out "They are?" Guiltily, I cover it with another question: "Your name is . . . ?"

"Mercy," she says. "I, you know, go by that. I started using it last year when I was dancing topless. Miss Mercy, they called me. Hey, c'mon, Thor! Leave the dude's shoe alone, man! Thor's kind of, you know, horny," she explains apologetically to Wig. "The lady dogs around here are all sort of too tall for him. He keeps tryin' to ball the cat, but she's like you, she's not too crazy about it either."

If Wig is wounded by the discovery that he is not the sole object of Thor's affection, he is too preoccupied just now to say so, what with trying to fend off both Thor's attentions to his foot and Jabbers's attentions to his bald noggin. "I jis wisht yawl'd looky here at the *head* on this ole boy, I b'lieve I never did see no ball-head hippie before, Yogurt and Whitey and them has got *plenny* hair but this here ole boy ain't got but jis that little ole *fuzz* around the *edge*, if you'd jis set *still* a minute and let ole Jabbers *rub* that head a little, we might could make hit *grow*, hee hee hee . . ."

"So," I inquire of Miss Mercy, "how long have you known these . . . beautiful dudes?"

"Oh, a *long* time, two or three months at *least*. They used to come in this place where I was a waitress. The Beast is from around here, I think. He's, like, a dropout. Yogurt and Wheatgerm are runaways from back East somewheres. Okaloma or somewheres."

Okies. The mind boggles.

"The thing is," Mercy goes on, "they're really penny-stricken, see. They live on just whatever they can hit people up for, and sleep just, you know, wherever they happen to crash, with a chick sometimes, or in the Beast's car. So like whenever I run into them I bring them home with me and feed them. I really love those three dudes, man, *truly* I do. I mean, they wouldn't've done anything like, you know, ripping off your shit or anything like that if they hadn't've been, you know, drunk."

"Drunk?" I am taken aback. "I thought they were . . . hippies."

"Oh, I guess they, you know, get stoned now and then, same as everybody else. But what they're really *into* is wine. They're juiceheads, mostly."

Despite my surprise, I have to concede, upon reflection, that this is actually one of the more cogent facts I've managed to glean about them—for I too have harkened upon occasion to the call of the wild grape. But I've been sort of reluctantly assuming, of recent years, that us juiceheads are a dying breed; and the shock of learning that we've merely been underground, just waiting to be rediscovered by the avant-garde, is almost too much for me. At last! A cultural revolution worth laying the old bod upon the line for!

"How about the Spirit?" I ask Miss Mercy. "Who's he?"

"I don't know too much about him," she says vaguely. "I think he's, like, a colored dude or something, maybe." She leans back and peers around the windowshade and exclaims, "Hey, there they are, they're back!"

The door crashes open out in the hall, Thor scrabbles hastily back under the couch, and in the blinking of an eye they have materialized before me, Yogurt and Wheatgerm and the Beast and the dog, all four of them grinning broadly and the dog wagging his tail besides, and dangling from the Beast's big right hand, which he is holding out to me, is my Hermes portable typewriter!

"Hey, far out, thanks, I . . ."

"Now, you ole Beasty, I don't reckon yawl would've brung ole Jabbers a li'l taste of Sneaky *Pete*, by any . . ."

"But it don't look too good for the radio, man," Wheatgerm is telling me, shaking his head sorrowfully. "Because the Spirit's got that, see."

What Wheatgerm is saying is, the Spirit ain't got quite as much respect for hip dudes as we do, see, so don't sit up nights waiting for him to bring your radio back. But so delighted am I to have made the grade as a hip dude, to have actually won admission to the august company of these splendid fellows, that at this point I couldn't possibly care less about the wretched radio. What's one radio more or less among us hip dudes? To hell with the radio! Let the radio go wherever the Spirit moves it!

"So tell me," I inquire of them, chuckling as merrily as if nothing in the world gratifies me quite so much as a good burglary at my own expense, "how'd you all break in my door?"

"Be damn if I can remember," the Beast admits, scratching his haymow reflectively. "We were drunk as dog shit, man."

"You *kicked* it down, you dumb fuck!" Wheatgerm crows. "You were so drunk you kicked the fucker right down, and can't even remember you did it!"

"Oh yeah, that's right, I did," the Beast muses, blushing modestly at the gargantuan proportions of his drunk.

"Hey listen, man," Yogurt says to me, "we really gotta get shakin', see. Because we have to get to this chick's house that said she'd ball us if we get there before her old man comes home from work. So we better split. We're sorry about your radio, though, man, we really are."

". . . I reckon this here's about the first ball-head hippie ever I run into . . ."

We are all on our feet now, and the Beast is shaking my hand again, and Wheatgerm and Yogurt are sort of plucking at my sleeves, imploring me one last time to forgive them for ripping off such a hip dude. And I, of course, am doing so with all my heart, trailing them halfway down the front hall dispensing absolution, feeling guilty as sin for stealing back my typewriter. For want of something better to offer them in recompense for the injustice of it all, I mention that I just might try to write something about them sometime.

"Good fucking deal, man," the Beast says heartily. "You can write anything you want to about me. 'Cause I can't read anyhow."

"Hey, Mercy," Yogurt calls back from the front door, "thanks a lot for the breakfast, man."

"Sure," she coos as the door slams after them. "Any time, man!"

I go back into the living room to gather up my typewriter and rescue Wig from Jabbers, who is again imploring permission to rub his pate (". . . it so *shiny*, jis lemme feel of it *one time*, hee hee hee . . ."), and from Thor, who is again putting the moves on the seductive desert boot. We are just maneuvering ourselves into position to make a break for it, when we hear the front door open, and suddenly the Beast is framed once more in the hall doorway.

"Hey listen, man," he says to me, "you ain't got any spare change you could lend us, have you?"

I come up with thirty-five or forty cents, which I'm half ashamed to offer him. But the Beast seems perfectly content with the donation.

"Thanks, man," he says cheerfully. "Later."

". . . hey, you ole Beasty you, if yawl gonna git some wine you won't forgit ole Jabbers, would you now, yawl 'member how ole Jabbers give yawl some Sweet Lucy the other day, you 'member that, don't you, Beasty . . ."

But Jabbers is too late, for the Beast is long gone once again. And this time Wig and I are close behind him.

"Bye bye," Miss Mercy calls sweetly as we slip out the door. "You dudes hurry back, now."

". . . shore, yawl come back I git you some nice vedgibles too, my ole woman she like to see a ole ball-head hippie, I take yawl home wimme . . ."

Wig and I reach the stoop just in time to see an old Ford ragtop pull away in a great cloud of blue exhaust. The dog is hanging half out of the gaping hole that used to be the back window, barking his head off, and the Beast and Yogurt are waving goodbye from the far side of the car, above the tattered top, and Wheatgerm is leaning out the window on the near side, his hands cupped to his mouth to make himself heard above the roar of the engine.

"Hey," he yells, "do you cats realize how *weird* all this shit is?"

"Sure we do," Wig says as the old car, listing and yawing, careens around the corner and out of sight. "We're in California, aren't we?"

So that afternoon I dropped in at the Palo Alto police station—the Pork Works, we local *illuminati* were fond of calling it—to report that, faced with the appalling incompetence of our appointed constabulary, I had conducted my own private investigation, had swiftly apprehended the typer-nappers with my bare hands, and, having discerned them to be, not unlike myself, members in good standing of the oppressed and voiceless masses, had liberated them to go forth and do the People's work. Or words to that effect. The impassive functionary behind the desk took down this intelligence without comment, and I left feeling, all things considered, enormously satisfied with myself. The hip dude had closed the case.

And I continued to feel pretty mellow right up until, late the same evening, as Wig and I were sitting up enjoying one last midnight pipe of Acapulco moonshine, the telephone rang and it was a Lieutenant Badger of the PAPD, who demanded to know, What means this nonsense in this report, Mr. Mickelhan, and wouldn't I like to clear up the record on this matter, and didn't I understand that after all a felony had been committed here, a *felony* Mr. Monahan, and I'm sure you understand that you can't just walk in here and halt an investigation of a felony, sir, merely because you personally happened to be fortunate enough to get your property back, don't you realize that there have been other burglaries of a similar nature in that neighborhood, and do you think it fair, Mr. Moneyhon, that your property should be returned to you whereas other persons have no hope of regaining theirs, don't you realize that the burglaries will continue until these people are brought to justice, it's too bad you don't feel you can cooperate with us, it's irresponsible citizens like you who make police work difficult, good evening, Mr. Asshole, click.

Unmanned by the rigor of the lieutenant's reproaches and the iron logic of his argument, I never even managed to get my defense mechanisms into

gear; my end of the dialogue sputtered along as if
my plugs were damp: Well, yessir, but . . . Yes,
that's so, but . . . I can understand that, but . . .
I see, but . . . Yes, but . . . Yes, but . . . Yes,
but . . .

He's right! I told Wig after I'd recounted Lt.
Badger's dressing-down. He's dead right; why
should I be immune from harm when my neighbors
are getting ripped off night after night? What kind
of world is it where the same mustache and hair
and granny glasses that almost got me dismantled
by Estill and Parky and Rickie-O had saved the day
for me with Yogurt and Wheatgerm and the Beast?
Was it really *that* far from the Penington Club to
the Poppycock?

"So," Wig ventured to interject, "you're going to
turn them in, then?"

What? Turn them in? Hand those beautiful dudes
over to the cops, after they trusted me enough to
confess their little indiscretion to me? C'mon, Wig!

"Well, maybe you should look them up and give
the typewriter back to them. Or"—Wig was grinning
now—"maybe you should just take an ax to the
typewriter and clear up the whole business once
and for all."

Then at last I got the point. Which is simply that
as long as there's a need to choose between love and
duty, there will be those who agonize that they cannot fully commit themselves to either. And their
hand-wringing shall become, in the end, itself a
kind of commitment. And they shall be called—

among other things, such as sophists, equivocators, cavilers, fucken punks, and even, now and then, hip dudes—they shall sometimes be called writers.

And that made me feel a little better about the whole deal—if only because it reminded me what I was supposed to do with the damned typewriter.

FIVE

Ken Kesey, Jean Genet, the Revolution, et Moi

"He is not a *tame* Lion."

—C. S. LEWIS, *The Last Battle*

I HOLD here before me a tattered and barely legible duplicate draft registration card, issued to me in August 1955, after I'd lost my original card, along with the rest of the contents of my billfold and the billfold itself, one night earlier that summer in a place called something like El Rancho Gringo in Nuevo Laredo, Mexico, under circumstances which, if I could remember them, I'd just as soon forget.

I've never been back to Nuevo Laredo, and never lost another billfold, so I've carried the duplicate ever since, although the fine print on the card advises me that I should have destroyed it as of my thirty-sixth birthday, more years ago than I care to count. I've hung on to it for sentimental reasons, rather the way one clings to the ticket stubs from some memorable concert or evening at the theater— for once upon a time, as a matter of fact on almost the very eve of that long-gone thirty-sixth birthday, I was sure that my old draft card was about to become my ticket to the glory of revolutionary martyrdom.

Indeed, I already had a lifelong history of flirtations with subversion. Was I not the only closet agnostic in Daily Vacation Bible School (having suffered a couple of boils myself at a tender age, I was privately of the opinion that Job had got the rawest kind of deal), and the only Marxist-Leninist-

Stalinist-Fascist Eisenhower Republican (this was purely for the sake of argument, you understand) in my freshman class at Washington & Lee, and the only proto-crypto-pseudo-semi-quasi-California Beatnik in the University of Kentucky English Department's graduate program in 1956? And wasn't I, in 1958, among the very first English instructors at Backwater State Teachers' College to sign the petition defending Gus Hall's right to speak on campus, despite the college president's assurance that this seditious act would pursue the signatories to their academic graves—which, he trusted, would prove both deep and early? Damn straight I was; don't mess with Robespierre, daddy-o.

So when I landed back in California in the 1960s, working the Visiting Lecturer in Creative Writing circuit, it was no surprise that in due time I could be observed on or about the premises of the institution we'd better call, hereinafter, the Harvard of the West, bedecked in peace symbols, love beads, Martin Luther King, Jr., memorial armbands, "Free Huey!" buttons, marching here, sitting-in there, protesting this, supporting that, locking horns with the Establishment wherever it reared its ugly reactionary head, Bakunin of the Suburbs, a bomb in my pocket and a slogan ever at the ready on my lips . . .

Truth to tell, I'm afraid I wasn't really cut out for the revolution business. Whenever I tried to chant "Ho-Ho-Ho Chi Minh!" or "Hey, hey, LBJ!" my tongue went limp, in an adamant little protest of its own. At demonstrations, I tended to wander dazedly from faction to faction, listening to the incessant arguments about goals, strategies, tactics, and whose-turn-is-it-to-go-for-Cokes until I was half drunk on other people's rhetoric, a lost soul seeking his Affinity Group. Once, during a rousing Stop-the-Draft riot outside the Oakland Induction Center, I gleefully set a curbside trash basket afire—and then, in a paroxysm of remorse, dashed through a traffic jam of police cars to the Doggy Diner across the street, slapped down a couple of quarters for a large Pepsi to go, dashed back across the street, and poured it on the blaze. There was, it seemed, a sort of spoilsport moral plumb bob somewhere inside me, an Automatic Equivocator that brought me back to perpendicular whenever it caught me listing too far to the left. I may have had the heart of a firebrand, but mah feets was moderate to the bone.

My career as a revolutionary reached its nadir that night in October 1968, just three days short of my thirty-sixth birthday, when I went all the way to Berkeley for the express purpose of torching my tattered old duplicate draft card at a huge hell-no-we-won't-go! rally on the hallowed steps of Sproul Hall, that most sacrosanct of Movement temples. I arrived with a headful of newsreel footage of how it was going to be: When they asked for volunteers, I'd be the first to come forward, an aging sacrificial lamb throwing his poor old body on the line just three days before it reached the safety of eternal deferment. Not that it wasn't perfectly safe already;

in fact, I'd been classified 4-F for years, thanks to a cooperative allergist who'd described my occasional hay fever as "chronic debilitating asthma" in a letter to my draft board. But my invulnerability merely added luster to the noble sacrifice I'd be making. For of course the government would have to prosecute such outright defiance; doubtless J. Edgar Hoover would dispatch his thugs to snatch me off to jail while the ashes of my draft card were still smoldering. "Free Ed!" the cry would ring across the land, ten thousand voices strong. "Free Ed! Free Ed!"

What actually happened, comrades, is that I stood around for hours, draft card in hand, listening to interminable speeches by a parade of posturing malingerers who were probably even more invulnerable to the draft than I was—and that at last, sometime around midnight, when the FBI had long since gone home to bed and the crowd had thinned out to the point that there weren't even enough warm bodies on hand to mount a respectable "Free Ed!" rally, someone passed among the stragglers with a metal wastebasket, collecting draft cards for the ritual immolation. I returned my card to my billfold, for a souvenir, and when the wastebasket came my way I tossed in an out-of-date fishing license instead. "Right on, man! Right on!" piped a couple of youthful voices here and there, with feeble enthusiasm. Following, for the first time since I outgrew *Crime Does Not Pay* comics, the good example of the FBI, I too went on home to bed.

From then on, my revolutionary ardor cooled considerably. I still dutifully showed up for marches and what-have-you, but I was just along for the walk; my heart wasn't in it anymore.

During the last days of 1969, as the Now Generation took its final tokes, there came into brief vogue the social phenomenon upon which Tom Wolfe was soon to pin the tag "Radical Chic," and in so doing to deal the fad a mortal wound, skewering it on the spot like some exotic but exceptionally short-lived butterfly.

Radical chic was, of course, that practice among prestigious, socially prominent people of throwing fund-and-consciousness-raising parties in their homes for the benefit of certain fashionable political causes—the antiwar movement, the civil-rights movement, the grape workers, the environmentalists . . . and, notably, the Black Panthers. The Panthers took New York penthouse society like Grant took Richmond; in fact, it was Leonard Bernstein's party for the Panthers that Wolfe would perforate with such fatal accuracy, in the famous essay first published in *New York* magazine in June 1970.

But for a while there, the Panthers were the hottest thing going, and a lot of loose change was being turned in the course of these curious fraternizings. So in early 1970, the Oakland chapter of the Panthers, who like Dickens's Mr. Bounderby could see as far into a grindstone as the next man, put together a traveling Panther-in-the-parlor act of their own, complete with a special imported extra-added attraction, the celebrated French pederast cutpurse incendiarist Marxist-Leninist writer and all-around fruitcake, Jean Genet, fresh out of prison for who-knows-what heinous offenses against whatever passes for human decency in France. They shipped Genet in by way of Toronto, where he laid over long enough to hold several press conferences in which he rather shrilly expressed his conviction that the FBI planned to snuff him the instant he set foot on American soil. The FBI didn't oblige him; when he landed in Oakland they evinced no more interest in him than they had in stopping the "Free Ed!" movement. Undaunted, the Panthers tricked him out in a tiny Panther Junior Auxiliary black leather jacket (Genet would wear about a boys' size 12), like some preposterous little mascot, and began exhibiting him around the neighborhood. Within a few days I got a phone call inviting me to a hastily arranged wine-and-cheese social that very afternoon at the home of an eminent Harvard of the West professor, to enjoy a warm excoriation of myself and selected other white liberal Enemies of the People, administered by those experts at the work, Jean Genet and the Black Panthers.

Which is where Ken Kesey comes into the picture.

Ken had long since left California to its own infernal devices and moved back to Oregon, but it so happened that when the party invitation came, he and I—Ken being between planes on his way home from Los Angeles—were sitting at my kitchen table

Ken Kesey, Jean Genet, the Revolution, et Moi

in Palo Alto, talking Black Panthers. A friend had recently taken him to a Panther rally, Ken's been telling me, and all the whites in attendance were subjected to a weapons shakedown at the door, a procedure which Ken's experience has taught him is demeaning to both parties, frisker and friskee alike.

"It's a cop trip," he insists, "and it's a big mistake. They shouldn't be trying to out-asshole the assholes, they should try to be the *good* guys."

He goes on to tell me how, up in Oregon, his brother Chuck's creamery business sponsors a basketball team in the local municipal league, and how there are a couple of spades (still a term of endearment among us diehard old hipsters) on Chuck's team, and how, one recent night, the team found itself involved in a game the referee of which was evidently persuaded that only black players committed fouls.

"So we all started callin' *him* on it," Ken says. "Whenever he called a foul on our guys, we'd jump up off the bench and call one on *him*. And pretty soon the crowd could see it too, and they got into it, everybody was on his case, and we shamed the guy till he *had* to call a straight game . . ."

Along about here the phone rings, with the invitation to the professor's at-home, to meet the winsome *enfant horrible*, as well as David Hilliard, the acting Exalted Grand Sachem of the Oakland Panthers (Bobby Seale, Huey P. Newton, and Eldridge Cleaver being either incarcerated, exiled, or otherwise indisposed at the moment). After I've hung up,

9 5

I explain the deal to Ken and ask him if he'd like to come along.

"Far out," he answers. "I'll wear your shirt."

Now, I realize that introducing a commonplace shirt into my narrative at this critical juncture risks trivializing the momentous issues with which we are concerned here. But this is *not* a commonplace shirt, this is my Frisco Fag-Store Bebop Buccaneer Blouse, my Polk Street Sike-O-Deelic Swashbuckler, the silky, silvery one with the shiny blue paisleys as big as quahogs and the mother-of-pearl buttons and the huge, billowy sleeves and the tight three-button cuffs and the cantilever collar and the gullet-to-sternum décolletage, my Saturday-Night-at-the-Fillmore shirt, which is even now hanging right there on the kitchen doorknob, where I hung it this morning when it came back from the dry cleaner. Ken has had his eye on it ever since he walked in. But does he really intend to wear *that* to a Panther party? He'll go over like a transvestite at a Green Beret reunion.

Well, he certainly does; he intends to wear—and he does wear—not just the shirt, but also his neon red-and-white-striped hip-hugger bells and his bug-eye blue reflector shades and his American-flag front tooth and his new twelve-tone hand-painted Day-Glo sneakers, a little something he's just picked up in L.A. He goes off and suits up in this insane ensemble, and when he comes back into the room, he looks so smashing that I applaud him, and declare on the spot that the shirt is his forevermore.

Ken Kesey, Jean Genet, the Revolution, et Moi

On our way out the front door we meet our mutual pal Gordon Fraser, the only dealer still in the business who actually sells an Original Lid—a Prince Albert can, stuffed good and snug. Naturally, we go right back in and buy one, and refresh ourselves accordingly. Soon we're off again, this time taking Gordon with us, over his protests: "Panthers? I dunno, wait a moment, wait a moment . . ." Gordon has pulled a couple of years in the Joint himself, and the prospect of fellowshipping with Black Panthers is not his idea of a good time. But he's game, and off we go—as a matter of fact in Gordon's car, just for the ambiance.

The Eminent Professor lives in the Harvard of the West faculty ghetto, a lavish suburb-within-the-suburbs just off the campus, where the university has installed some of the finest minds of Western civilization, on the theory that if you put a fine mind in a nice Eichler split-level, it will sit right down and get busy thinking important thoughts. We know we're at the right house when we spot what have to be Panthermobiles—a matched pair of sleek black Citroëns with photo-gray no-see-um windows —parked at the curb outside.

We are met at the garden gate by the resident fine mind's minion, his graduate teaching assistant, who is checking a guest list, to keep out the riffraff that commonly prowl the faculty ghetto streets. I happen to know this particular grad student; he's notorious on campus for calling everybody over thirty "Doctor"—textbook salesmen, typewriter repairmen, grounds keepers—just in case. Now he stands there all agog, with his chin on his chest and his pencil frozen above his checklist, as Ken, blazingly resplendent in the brilliant California afternoon, strides past him as though he were part of the shrubbery. Gordon follows Ken, but the grad student never even notices him.

"I know you're on the list, Dr. McClanahan," he gulps when he finds his voice, "but who—?"

"That's Dr. Kesey," I tell him. "He's with me."

"Ken Kesey!" he cries happily. "Oh wow! Wait'll I go tell Dr. Cheesewitz! Ken Kesey!" He scurries off into the garden, rubbing his hands together as if (as Tom Wolfe likes to put it) he's making invisible snowballs.

Inside the gate, a fairly good-sized party, maybe forty or fifty people, has assembled itself on the lawn and is tucking into the wine and cheese with an excellent appetite and chatting convivially with itself. Mostly, I note as I hurry after Ken and Gordon, they're folks I know, at least by sight if not by name, junior faculty and wives and grad students and, here and there, the odd progressive young lawyer, doctor, dentist, or Unitarian minister; the crowd that always turns out for the milder, more restrained rallies, nice, earnest liberals whose greatest happiness is in marching along arm in arm under the "Concerned Citizens" banner, singing "We Shall Overcome" with revolutionary fervor. Senior faculty —except for our host, the estimable Dr. Cheesewitz, who is at this very moment approaching me through the crowd with his hand already extended in greeting—is largely unrepresented here today.

"How do you *do*, Mr. Mackrelham!" exclaims Dr. Cheesewitz, pumping my hand warmly as he peers over my shoulder, looking for Ken. "*So* good of you to come! Mumford here"—out of nowhere the graduate student materializes beside him, manufacturing snowballs at a phenomenal rate—"Mumford here tells me you've brought us . . . ah, Mr. Kesey!"

Ken has turned, and now he looms prodigiously before us, as gaudy and gorgeous as a Christmas tree. For just the merest moment, you could knock Dr. Cheesewitz's eyeballs off with a broomstick. But he recovers quickly and grabs Ken's hand, prattling, "*Awfully* good of you to come, Mr. Kesey! I've admired *Some Fell Out of the Cuckoo's Nest* for years! *So* pleased to meet you, *so* nice to have you, *such* an unexpected pleasure!"

Ken is suffering these effusions politely, but he is not moved to say how delighted he is to be here, or what a wonderful time he's having. A bit desperately, the professor turns to Mumford. "Aren't we fortunate, Mumford, in having *two* famous authors with us?"

"Fame," Ken says. "Let me tell you about fame." Dr. Cheesewitz leans attentively toward him, waiting. "Fame," says Ken solemnly, "is a wart."

"A . . . wart," the professor repeats. He waits, but Ken is inscrutable behind his Plastic Man shades, and no elaboration is forthcoming. "Hmm, yes, a wart. Just so. Ha ha. That's *very* good. 'Fame is

. . . a wart.' Isn't that good, Mumford? Say there, Mumford, be a good fellow, won't you, and take Mr. Kesey and his friends over to meet our"—he hesitates, as if something in him balks at the encomium—"our guest of honor. Thank you so much, Mumford . . ." Dr. Cheesewitz turns away and drifts off into the crowd, shaking his head distractedly.

Mumford, bowing and scraping like a Chinese headwaiter, leads us toward a little clutch of people gathered in the far corner of the yard, Gordon and I bringing up the rear, Gordon murmuring "Wait a moment, wait a moment!" all the way. At the fringes of the little assembly, the crowd falls away from Ken as if, bedazzled, they fear they'll be struck blind by so much splendor, and I see that the center of attention is—or was, until Ken got there—one very small, very pale, very unprepossessing Frenchman, bald as your thumb, flanked by two very large, very dark, very imposing Black Panthers, all three decked out in matching Panther leathers and the two big bodyguards in black berets as well, like . . . like an *act*, see, like Gladys Knight and the Pips, or The Two Hits and a Miss. There's even a backup group behind them, half a dozen more uniformed Panthers, among whom I recognize David Hilliard, and a thin young white woman with rimless glasses, a pinched look about the mouth, and her hair pulled back so severely into a bun that the circulation to her nose is apparently compromised—for its tip is already turning a frosty white. This fetching dose

of salts—Mlle Deadbolt, let's call her—is with us
today courtesy of a Berkeley cell of feminist Maoists,
to translate for M. Genet, who has no English.

The two bodyguards glare balefully at Ken as he
approaches, but Genet is goggle-eyed; in France they
haven't seen this much finery since the Folies-
Bergère moved to Vegas. Ignoring the Panthers,
Ken plants himself before the diminutive prodigy,
grins a big warm friendly American grin—complete with a tiny American flag smack in the center
of it!—thrusts out his hand, and announces, in the
extra-large voice that most of us employ when ad-
dressing foreigners, "I'm Kesey!"

Genet manages a wan smile and a limp handshake,
but it is plain he has no idea under heaven what a
kee-zee is, or why they get themselves up this way.

"And this"—Mumford is doing the honors—"is
Dr. McClanahan and, uh . . ."

"Dr. Fraser," I put in, as Gordon reluctantly
comes forward. "He's in the Pharmacology Department."

The larger and more menacing of the two bodyguards taps Mumford smartly on the shoulder and
commissions him to "run an' git M'shoo Je-nay a
little glass of that Boojalaize." Mumford doesn't
need to be told twice; he excuses himself and scuttles
off.

Genet, having shaken hands all around, rocks back
on his heels to find Ken still rooted there before him,
grinning resolutely. Who is this *grand bouffon*, Genet
is surely wondering, and why does he not move

along? Ken, meanwhile, is just as surely thinking, Now if I could just take this weird little booger aside and explain to him, straight from the shoulder, famous author to famous author, jailbird to jailbird, baldhead to baldhead, about how the Panther trip is a cop trip, about how they shouldn't try to out-asshole the assholes, about how up in Oregon my brother Chuck's creamery's basketball team . . .

So there they stand, Ken with his arms folded over his great paisley chest, Genet fidgeting somewhere beneath him, shuffling his feet, glancing furtively about in search of someone else to shake hands with, rolling his eyes heavenward, only to find a whole paisley skyscape grinning down upon him, hastily lowering his gaze to the ground, where it lights upon—*Zut alors! Quels sabots!*—the twelve-tone hand-painted Day-Glo L.A. sneakers!

"L.A.!" Ken says expansively, still in his heartiest all-foreigners-are-deaf voice. "Los An-je-lus! L.A.!"

"Eh? Los . . . ?" Suddenly Genet brightens. "Los Angeles! Eh? Eh? Los Angeles!" Ken nods, urging him on, whereupon Genet points to his own feet—he wears the cunningest little tan Hush Puppies, brand-spanking-new ones—and squeaks, "*To-ron-to!*"

Unfortunately, we have only just arrived at this breakthrough in international understanding when Mumford returns with a paper cup of wine for Genet, and word that it's discussion-and-castigation time, and that Dr. Cheesewitz proposes we gather in the living room, where we are to hear a prepared statement by Genet and get what's coming to us.

Genet is quickly led away by his handlers, and the rest of the crowd drifts after them. Ken and Gordon go on inside, but I peel off at the front door and veer across the deck for the wine bar and a little last-minute taste of Boojalaize. On the way I meet my friend and cohort Fred Nelson, who is covering the occasion for *The Free You,* of which he is managing editor and guiding genius. Fred is carrying a tape recorder.

"Why don't you encourage Kesey to get into the discussion?" he suggests, with a cagey eye to spicing up his story.

I decline the honor in a hurry, pretty well satisfied that the Panthers wouldn't find the Springfield Creamery basketball team parable all that edifying. But I don't imagine Ken will require much encouragement, if it comes to that.

By the time I've wined myself up and found my way into the house, Dr. Cheesewitz's living room is knee deep in white liberals sitting on the carpet, with Genet perched in an immense La-Z-Boy in the far corner of the room, imperious as the frog prince on his throne. To either side of him is a couch, upon which is seated a rank of unsmiling Panthers. At Genet's feet hunkers Mlle Deadbolt, looking snappish, and to his immediate left sits David Hilliard, a large, dark, dour man with a handsome black leather attaché case across his knees. The entertainment is in progress, with a vengeance; young Dr. Chutney, an assistant professor of sociology with an immense Tolstoyan beard, is on his legs before the fireplace, reading aloud from the translation of Genet's prepared malediction. I spot Ken and Gordon standing in a little alcove off the rear of the room and ease myself over to join them.

The statement is a lengthy one, all cant, rant, and invective, undefiled by any taint of grace or wit or sense. We are, Genet is here to tell us, a nation of white racists, wherein the "dominating caste," the police, is in cahoots with the Mafia to distribute drugs to black people, the better to oppress them; we terrorize our intellectuals, as evidenced by the fact that the Harvard of the West has yet to offer Eldridge Cleaver a professorship; we are white slave drivers, colonialists; we are either pawns or perpetrators of the international banking conspiracy; we'd better stop the trial of Bobby Seale, or else; if we don't arm ourselves and take to the streets *tout de suite*, we're in a fair way to get our white academic asses handed to us on a silver salver, come the Revolution.

Throughout Dr. Chutney's spirited rendition of these (and many similar) compliments, their amiable author sits bolt upright, darting quick, avid little glances about the room as though he were hungry and looking for flies. When Dr. Chutney finishes his number and throws the floor open for discussion, Genet is first to speak, his voice shrill, hectoring, and incantatory:

104

Ken Kesey, Jean Genet, the Revolution, et Moi

"Vous intellectuels, vous professeurs, donnez-moi une leçon! Si vous n'êtes pas d'accord avec . . ."

"You intellectuals, you professors," echoes Mlle Deadbolt, with equal rancor, "give me a lesson! I begin by accusing the people in this room! Your power isn't great, but it's comfortable power! You are the accomplices of the great American banks and corporations that dominate the world! If you do not agree, correct me *right now*, so I can rectify it!"

("Wait a moment," Gordon murmurs, "wait a moment, wait a moment!" Beside him, Ken stands the way he always stands, stock-still, as intransigently stationary as a statue of himself. Inside his head, the creamery basketball team has already begun to rally.)

"A good professor cannot give a lesson, but can learn a lesson," Dr. Chutney is venturing to observe, reverently but unfathomably, from the abject prostration into which he seems to have collapsed upon the carpet. "So I, for one, am here to get a lesson."

Genet promptly takes up the lash again—*"Faites attention! Vous intellectuels, vous êtes complices de . . ."*—and proceeds to administer Dr. Chutney and his fellows a lesson in humility they will not soon forget.

And for a time, this exchange—vituperative tongue-lashing answered by craven whimper—sets the tone and pattern of the discussion period. The more enthusiastically Genet reviles the assembled champions of democracy, the more meekly they— all right, *we*—receive the indictment; we know we must be guilty, because we *feel* guilty all the time. Even when Genet acknowledges, proudly, that his credentials as a revolutionary derive from his having been sent to prison for theft, it is we who are somehow made to take the blame, as though we were the thieves ourselves. Our scourge, meanwhile, is having the time of his life; the words fly from his mouth like tiny bats, shrill and malevolent. He never knew Americans were so much fun.

But every worm has his turning point, and after Genet and Mlle Deadbolt have favored us with fifteen or twenty minutes of friendly exhortation, someone —Mumford? Could that be Mumford?—dares to inquire who is financing Dr. Genet's current adventure in international diplomacy. Genet replies, with a Gallic sniff, that his books and plays have brought him "a little fortune," which, he seems to suggest, he has placed entirely at the disposal of Bobby Seale, Ho Chi Minh, and Chairman Mao. *Toutefois*, he goes on, we should not allow ourselves to be sidetracked by such trivial concerns, we should instead be concentrating on saving the Black Panther Party from the savage clutches of the bloodthirsty American judiciary.

But how *do* you stop a trial? Mumford—hanging in there—wants to know. Why, Dr. Chutney volunteers, you simply put thousands of people in the streets, like at the Moratorium, and you . . . Okay, someone else breaks in, but then what happens when . . . Now, as Mlle Deadbolt struggles frantically to catch up, little arguments break out like

chicken pox in several corners of the room at once:
"Well, I don't think that by arming and by violence
you can . . ." "This country's going completely
Fascist, and . . ." "But they'd get wiped out,
if . . ." "Now at the Moratorium, they . . ."

"ORDER!"

The resounding imperative has issued from David
Hilliard, who accompanies it by hammering on his
attaché case with a fist like a three-pound lump of
anthracite. Hilliard's been around these scenes
enough to know that intellectuals tend to be more
tractable when they can be prevented from squab-
bling among themselves. And when he wants order,
he gets order; the room is suddenly as still as a
moment of silent prayer.

"We are not here today," he says at length, in a
voice that would freeze vodka, "to waste words
tryin' to tell you people what to do, 'cause we know
you're not gonna do it." Eldridge, he reminds us,
busted his hump running around talking to professors and intellectuals, and what did it get him?
He got ran out of the country, that's what. Anyhow,
it is the judgment of history and the considered
opinion of the Black Panther Party that this country
ought to take a good bloodbath every so often,
whether it needs it or not. Fortunately for those of
us here today, there's a nice class struggle coming
up any minute now, but we'd better step lively if we
want to get into it on the winning side.

"You have to pick up guns," he admonishes this
roomful of desperados, most of whom would sooner

shoot themselves than point a gun at someone else, "and you have to move against the criminals, against the disturbers of the peace, against the lawbreakers! And *that*"—he deals the attaché case a heavy blow, the first of five—"is your *judges*, your po-lice *of*ficers, and your other *sym*bols of the *state!*"

Well, that does it. "Wait a moment!" Gordon exclaims, out loud this time, and I turn to see Ken step forth from his alcove and, heedless even of besmirching his Day-Glo sneakers with white liberal guilt, intrepidly wade in among the supine pedagogues, saying, "Let me tell you about the Springfield Creamery basketball team . . ."

Vainly, Hilliard tries to cut him off. "I think we should stick to serious . . ."

"Now my brother has a creamery up there in Springfield, and there's a basketball team, and the team is made up of my friends and my brother and people I know well, and . . ."

"Order! Order!" Hilliard beats a furious tattoo on the hapless attaché case. "I think we should stick to . . ."

"So these two spades from up there, these two Negroes up there that I know well, they were . . ."

"Get out of here!" shrieks Hilliard. "We didn't come here to talk crazy, we came here to talk about . . ."

"No, let me go through with it now, let me . . ."

Hilliard is on his feet, shaking the attaché case menacingly at Ken. "We will leave if this man continues to . . ." Beyond Hilliard, Genet's eyes are as big as teacups, rendering him even froggier than before.

"So the referee started calling fouls, and he was calling them heavy on the color . . . —on the black people, right? And so everybody there could see it, they could *see* it! As soon as a foul was called, it was right there where they could . . ."

Pandemonium! If some faculty ghetto anarchist had chucked a bomb through Dr. Cheesewitz's picture window, it could hardly have cleared the room any more efficiently. By the time Ken is ten words into his narrative, everybody in the place is making for the door—first Hilliard, screaming "Let's go! Let's go!" as he storms out; then Genet's two bodyguards, hoisting their small, staring charge between them with such rigor that his little Hush Puppies barely touch the floor; then Mlle Deadbolt, who glowers at Ken as if she'd like to bite him; then the rest of the Panthers, several of whom angrily declare, in passing, their aversion to all forms and manifestations whatsoever of jiveass red-neck honky intellectual bullshit; and, finally—as the air is rent by the racket of Citroën doors slamming, Citroën engines revving, Citroën tires squealing—come milling masses of bewildered academics all a-twitter, entreating one another to explain what on earth just happened. Among the last to leave is Ken himself, pursuing his analogy right out the door and into the front yard, trailed by Mumford and a small but rapt band of listeners.

"We blew the whistle on *him,* see, and when the

fans got on his case it took his power away. More of his Fascism had showed, see, than he had known was there! And from then on we had the game won, because . . ."

Most of the guests are heading for their cars, but a few little knots of people have gathered here and there on the front walk, Talking It Over, as academics will. Dr. Chutney is still skulking around behind his whiskers, looking unfulfilled, but when he mutters something to the effect that the famous Ken Kesey now stands revealed as a reactionary racist swine, one of his brother savants immediately scoffs, Oh, come off it, Chutney, and that's the last we hear from the Sociology Department.

"So the real power of the movement thing, the civil-rights thing, is way up there in the back row. But the Panthers, now, they can't generate that sort of response, that affection that gets the back row to rooting *for* them instead of . . ."

While Ken, by sheer doggedness and main strength, pulls the analogy to earth and finishes it off, Gordon comes over to say that if I can line myself up another ride, he'll drive Ken directly to the airport to catch his plane. Sure, I tell him, Mumford there will run me home.

". . . And our job," Ken says, wrapping it up, "is to watch the ref and keep him honest. But overthrowing the law, the *idea* of the law in its pure form, that's a mistake. Because without the ref, see, you can't play the game."

"Mr. Kesey," asks Mumford eagerly, "do you

think the Panthers really wanted to . . . to have a dialogue with us? Because otherwise, why didn't they stay and talk?"

"I think," says Ken, "that they were looking for a bunch of zombies. And some of us"—he bestows his fabled, flag-bedizened all-American grin on Mumford, a regular Medal of Honor of a grin—"some of us just didn't qualify."

Moments later, Mumford and I stand together on the sidewalk watching Ken and Gordon pull away in Gordon's little yellow VW Beetle, with the smoke already rolling from its windows.

"Wow, Dr. McClanahan," Mumford giggles, as they buzz off into the sunset, "who *was* that masked man?"

"Mumford," I tell him happily, "that was no ordinary man, that was the leader of the Free Ed movement."

In memoriam Gordon Fraser, d. 1977.

SIX

Little Enis: An Ode on the Intimidations of Mortality

LAWYER:
Yer Honor, my client Joe Hogbristle
wants to change his name.
JUDGE:
Well, I can certainly understand that.
What does he want to change it to?
LAWYER:
He wants to change it to Fred
Hogbristle. Says he's tired of people
saying, "Hello, Joe, whaddya know!"

—*1001 Jokes for All Occasions*

down guitar in Rockabilly Heaven. But that, as they say, is another story—or several other stories, actually. Enough for now that we get some of the loose ends of this one untangled.

As far as my part in it is concerned, it began one night in the fall of 1956 in Lexington, Kentucky, when I walked into the Zebra Bar—a musty, murky coal-hole of a place across Short Street from the Drake Hotel (IF YOU DUCK THE DRAKE YOUR A GOOSE!! read the peeling roadside billboard out on the edge of town)—walked in under a marquee that did, sure enough, declare the presence inside of one "Little Enis," and came upon this amazing little stud stomping around atop the bar, flailing away at one of those enormous old electric guitars that looked like an Oldsmobile in drag—left-handed! He's playing it left-handed! And upside down besides!—this pugnacious-looking little banty rooster with a skin-tight gold-sateen cowboy shirt and an underslung lower jaw and a great sleek black-patent-leather Elvis Presley pompadour and long Elvis Presley sideburns and a genuine Elvis Presley duck's-ass (*You know, people sometimes asks me what I think of these people like you, which has got the long hair and all. And I just say, Well, they've got their thing to do. Because actually, see, I've had long hair my own self since I was fifteen years old. I mean, I was the first one that created long sideburns in Lexington! I had 'em down to here!*), this five-foot four-inch watch-fob knickknack of an Elvis up there just a-stompin' and a-flailin', laying down a rendition of

"Blue Suede Shoes" that would have done the master proud. In fact, he was even (oh, blasphemy!) *better* than Elvis, his guitar playing distinctly saltier, his inflections ("You c'n do enny*thang* that y'wanna *dew* / But onh-onh, honey, lay *offa* my shews!") just a shade flatter, twangier, down-homier, his bump 'n' grind at least as lewd and spirited as anything the Big E himself had thrown at us on *Ed Sullivan* a few Sundays back. We all flashed to him instantly, and hastened to settle our sodden selves into a booth so that my roommate, Willie Gordon Ryan, the evening's patron live one, could spring us to the opening round.

We. That would have included, let's see, Ryan, who was in college at last after a four-year hitch in the Air Force (as a matter of fact, that's what we were celebrating that night; it was the day Ryan's monthly GI Bill check came in), and several well-saturated running mates of ours, Tommy Cook and I. J. Wagner and Little Billy Whealdon and Buster Kline and . . .

And me, which is the beginning to a whole other loose end, the loosest end of all, some might say. For this was but a few months after my triumphant return from my first stint at the Harvard of the West, where, I'll remind you, I had distinguished myself by flunking out of graduate school. So I hadn't come home with that old sheepskin to nail to the wall, but I did bring back my armpit goatee and my spaniel's-ass haircut and my shades and Levi's and cycle boots, in which Califinery I currently orna-

mented the campus of the University of Kentucky—
where I was flunking out of graduate school. Already
I ranked right up there with Adolph Rupp's round-
ball coliseum and the Agricultural Experiment
Station among the sights not to be missed on the UK
campus. On football weekends, whole carloads of old
grads would screech to a halt in heavy traffic to stare
and point; fraternity men's upper lips automatically
curled into sneers the instant I came into view;
sorority housemothers hastened to gather their
maidenly charges behind their skirts at the very mention of my name.

But now about this Toadvine. Well, in a way, he
saved my graduate career, such as it was. Because
up until the moment I walked into the Zebra Bar
that night, I'd been persuaded that there was no
way in the world I could stand Lexington long
enough to get my M.A. and, as the saying went,
make like a sewer and get the shit out of there.
Maybe I'd just chuck the whole deal, I told myself
darkly, and join the army, where they knew how to
appreciate us nonconformists. But suddenly there
he was, Little Enis, all the evidence I could ask for
that even out here in the unillumined heart of the
provinces, careful inspection was liable to turn up
some cultural phenomenon worthy of an enlightened
man's condescension.

Enis took to flattery like a duck to water, poor
innocent. All I had to do was buy him a seventy-five-
cent Zebra Zombie at his first break between sets,
and advise him that, as a noted folklorist from the

university (where, in fact, I was currently pulling a low C in the only folklore course I ever enrolled in), I was satisfied that he and his understudy Elvis constituted the single most cosmic event in the history of American ethnosecular music (a genre which I invented on the spot), and that I was prepared to embark on a study of him which was a cinch to make us both as famous as Silly Putty. And that was it; I had me an Artifact to patronize. My military future would have to be postponed.

For the next two or three weeks, I paid court to Enis at the Zebra as often as I could finance a field trip down to Short Street. When he left the Zebra and hired on at Martin's, a breathtakingly unsanitary country-and-Western tavern over on the north side of town, I took my trade there too—at some peril, I might add, for the clientele at Martin's tended to look at me unsociably out of the corners of their eyes. And when Enis moved on to the Palms, a plywood-and-glass-brick *moderne* cocktail lounge between a drive-in theater and a varmint-burger stand out on the Northern Beltline, I practically took up residence in the place.

Now, the Palms had lately fallen into the hands of a certain Linville Puckett, who until that very autumn had been an almost-All-American guard on the UK basketball team, but who had come to a parting of the ways with Baron Rupp—some small dispute over training rules, as I recall—and had turned in his jock and moved around to the business side of the bar, to become a night-life impresario. He'd taken over this dingy roadhouse, complete with the pair of dusty plastic potted palm trees that flanked the ladies' room door, and renamed it Linville Puckett's Palms, and installed the slickest dance floor in town and the liveliest jukebox in town and the hottest attraction in town, which was my excellent friend Little Enis and his new combo, the Fabulous Tabletoppers. (*Yeah, they was quite a few stars out there at that time. I was about the biggest thing in Lexington, so they would all say I was a big star, and Linville, he was a basketball star. So that was quite a good drawin' card, Linville Puckett, the All-American basketball player, and Little Enis, the All-American Left-Handed Upside-down Guitar Player.*) Within a week the Palms was jumping every night, Puckett's most avid admirers showing up right after work when he was usually tending bar, early enough to drink their suppers, blue-collar sports fans and UK fratties drunkenly maneuvering for choice barstools all through vespers, hoping to hear the defrocked Wildcat tell how he'd told Der Baron he could take his basketball and shove it up his coliseum. By around eight o'clock Enis would generally have joined them at the bar, knocking back a few whiskey-and-Cokes or a couple of cool ones to clear his head before the first set. (*When I was drinkin', I'd live each day from day to day, that's how I lived during my drinkin' years. And when I'd go to sleep I wouldn't even think about gettin' up. And then the next day I'd get up and party again.*

Little Enis: The Intimidations of Mortality

I finally went out here to Eastern State Hospital to
get me some help. That shrinker said to me, "Are you
a alcoholic?" And I said, "Well, if you call drinkin'
a quart of whiskey before you can read the Sunday
paper a alcoholic, then I reckon I must be one.")

Along about eight-thirty the guys with dates would
be falling by, here a Deke out a-slumming with his
Tri Delt, there a TV repairman hustling the wife
of a client who worked the night shift at the Dixie
Cup factory; and by a little after nine maybe a few
unattached girls would have turned up, telephone
operators and typists from the IBM typing pool
and students from the Fugazzi Business College and
the Vine Street Academy of Beauty, gathering themselves in jittery little coveys here and there at tables
closest to the dance floor, where the light was better.
They'd sit there glaring at those oblivious stiffs
crowded around the bar until finally one of them,
say an aspiring beautician working on her Ph.D. in
beehives at the academy, would get so pee-oh'd she'd
pick up her Tom Collins and sashay over to the
jukebox and plug it with her own quarter, punching
out maybe "Fever," and "Raunchy," and Elvis's
latest, "Paralyze"; and when Little Willie John
suddenly whumped out those few heavy bass notes
and growled "Never know how mu-uch I love you!"
the guys at the bar would look up, startled, to discover that the night was as young as the day was
old, and immediately begin to undergo the meta-
morphosis from sports fans to just plain sports,

their eyeballs ticking off their calculations like Rupp's new electronic scoreboards as they checked out the action in the other room.

By the time "Raunchy" was half over there'd be four or five newly acquainted couples on the dance floor, raunching away, doing a sort of post-jitterbug, pre-twist bop, standing there at arm's length grimacing and hunching their pelvises at each other in a kind of dirty-boogie face-off ("I jus' cain't *stand* that awful ole niggery dancin' they do out there!" a UK sorority girl once wailed to I. J. Wagner), and while Elvis was groaning his way through "Paralyze," Enis and the Fabulous Tabletoppers—a wonderful sax honker named Bucky Sallee, and a piano player named Frank, and a guy named either Johnny or Jerry on drums—would mount the bandstand beside the jukebox and start tuning up. As Elvis wrapped it up and Enis, cradling his guitar in that weird way of his and grinning an utterly wicked, lickerish grin, stepped forward into the Palms' feeble greenish-yellow spotlight, his pompadour glinting like obsidian, his tidy little torso all a-shimmer in the gold-sateen cowboy shirt, his tiny white hands poised above the first fleet notes of "All Shook Up" (*Well, my daddy was a farmer in Hogue Holler, over here by Danville, and I swear he couldn't play the reddy-o without gettin' static on it. But my mother, she sung in church, and I'd've walked a country mile to hear her sing a song, she had the most beautiful voice you ever heard. And her people, they was entertainers, years ago they was with Red*

Little Enis: The Intimidations of Mortality

Foley at Renfro Valley. My uncle, he was the state fiddlin' champion on the old breakdown fiddle at the state fair. So they would all get together of a Sunday afternoon, and everybody'd bring their music instruments, and I was just a little thing, y'know, but I'd santer around th'oo that crowd and directly I'd pick up somebody's guitar, and the first thing you know I'd be a-bangin' on it!), stepped forward into the Palms' blare and reek, and with the spotlight glaring in his eyes, the only thing he could make out would be . . .

Me again. The old loose end again, the noted folklorist again, drunk again. Sitting there right under Enis's nose at the table nearest the bandstand, wearing those ridiculous shades and that ridiculous Levi's suit and that ridiculous haircut, drunk as a lord since three o'clock in the afternoon, when I had inconspicuously departed from my Romantic Poetry seminar at the tea-and-cookies break and had fled to the revolting pigsty of an apartment I shared with Willie Gordon Ryan upstairs over the Southern Girl Beauty Salon, and had found Ryan there busily cutting freshman English, and had straightway sallied forth once more with Ryan at my side, as faithful a Sancho Panza as e'er a Quixote could've asked for (it being the day *my* check came in, bearing my father's customary reluctant-looking signature), to an establishment called the Paddock Club, where we drank Oertels '92 beer straight through till seven-thirty, excepting one time out for a fried baloney sandwich, and where I had once again made

a jackass of myself by authoritatively informing
some indignant coed that the doodles in the back of
her *Family and Marriage* textbook revealed "a defi-
nite tendency toward the Freudian concept we call
penis envy." And also where I. J. Wagner and
Tommy Cook, on their way home to study for a
Poultry Management exam after a leisurely dinner
of beer and pickled eggs and pinball at the Scott
Hotel Bar, dropped by for a spot of Oertels '92, just
to clear their palates, and from which the three of
us (Sancho Ryan having already committed his iron
to other fires that night) repaired forthwith to the
Palms, I.J. and Cookie to juice some more and dance
them niggery dances and hustle the ladies a bit; I
to do my noted folklorist act—dancing is not my
strong suit—for the third time that week. And to
juice some more.

Thus had I arrived at my present sorry state,
drumming my thumbs against the tabletop with
inebrious, a-rhythmical abandon, while on the bandstand just above me Little Enis, his feet planted in
that classic Presley straddle, his groin thrusting like
the machine-tooled private parts of the Great Fucking Wheel, his left leg jiggling spasmodically inside
his pants as if he really *was* a-eetchin' lak a bug on
a fuzzy tree, tore like a man possessed into Elvis's
repertoire, *segue*ing out of "All Shook Up" straight
into "Hound Dog," then laying back ever so slightly
with "Teddy Bear" (the lively lovelies of the Palms
squealed like bobby-soxers over that one—because,
as I overheard one of them sigh when Enis purled

"Run yo' fangers th'oo mah hair an' cuddle up real tight!" and hove a lusty dry-hump in her direction, "I could cuddle *that* sweet thing to *death*!"), then cranking it up again with "Blue Suede Shoes" and, for variety, Little Richard's "Long Tall Sally" and Fats Domino's "Kansas City," then tying off the set with a "That's When Your Heartaches Begin" so mellow and lachrymose that Colonel Parker would have shed a tear in his Hadacol if he'd been there to hear it.

And through it all there sat the Palms' own noted folklorist and resident greaser, thumping away at my tabletop like a tone-deaf Sal Mineo auditioning for *The Gene Krupa Story*, applauding furiously for every number, calling out requests at the top of my voice between songs—"Hey, Enis, do 'Rip It Up'! Do 'Jailhouse Rock'! Do 'Hound Dog' again!"— generally pulling out all the stops, so that he would come and sit at my table during his break and let me buy an Oertels '92 and patronize him some.

Oh, there were plenty of times when a tableful of admiring Palmettes would snag him first ("That little son-of-a-buck will get laid where most men couldn't get a drink of water," a Palms bartender confided to me one night. "I heard a couple of these old girls say he's *awful* heavy hung. They was talking about somebody named Old Blue, and it turned out they was referring to Enis's pecker!"); but for all their charms, they were wanting in that sophisticated appreciation of his Art that he could always depend on finding at my table. So at least once or twice an evening he'd join me—and, if the pickings on the dance floor were running slim, I.J. and Cookie—for a quick one, and I'd tell him how he was the biggest thing in troubadouring since Allan-a-Dale, and he'd tell me about all the offers he was getting from Dot Records, and all the albums they were begging him to cut, and all the road tours he was going on . . . and one night, when my panegyrics had left him in an especially expansive mood, he confided that he was temporarily working days as a "maintenance engineer," shoveling coal into the LaFayette Hotel's furnace, and that his real name was Carlos Toadvine. He never did quite get my name, by the way; his best effort was the time he introduced me to a barmaid as "Ted Flannigan, he's gettin' his doctor degree on my life story, out at the colletch."

Throughout that fall and early winter I was liable to drop by the Palms as often as three or four nights a week to pay my respects to Enis; it got so the waitresses would deliver an Oertels '92 to my ringside table as soon as I walked in the door. Then in January I finally met a Lexington girl who, although her tastes in music were a good deal tonier than mine (the first present I ever gave her was a 45 of Chuck Berry's "Roll Over, Beethoven"), was content to sit there while I rattled our beer glasses with my tattooing thumbs (the first present she ever gave me was a set of bongo drums) and told her about the master's thesis I planned to write, au-

daciously entitled "The Influence of the Celtic Bardic
Tradition upon the Work of Carlos Toadvine."

Fortunately for the general state of belles lettres,
I never got around to writing it; because in the
spring of '57 there occurred the two most momentous events of my young life: I got married, and I
flunked my master's oral. Flunked it cold as a
wedge; I hadn't been in that room with those three
professors fifteen minutes before my California cool
had turned into an iceberg on my tongue. I couldn't
have told them so much as the date of the Battle
of Hastings—much less who fought it, or who won.
Get a grip on yourself, McClanahan, the trio of
professors chorused sternly, shaking their hoary
heads in unison; quit hanging around bars pre-
tending to be some kind of Beatster or whatever
they call it, and start applying yourself to the study
of the history of English literature, and come back
next year and try again.

Shaken to my very cycle boots, I did as I was told:
I put in a whole year writing a master's thesis au-
daciously entitled "A Selective Bibliography of
Critical Approaches to the Poetry of Robert Brown-
ing, 1935–1950," and sitting in on sophomore literature surveys, memorizing names and dates and titles
and the rhyme schemes of the sonnet. True, I didn't
altogether abandon my old identity: every now and
then I'd suit up in my Beatster best (except for the
goatee, which had gone down the drain of the Southern Girl Beauty Salon apartment's bathroom sink on

the morning of my wedding day) and drop by the
Palms and trade a little fried baloney with old Enis.
But it wasn't the same, somehow; my head had got so
full of titles and dates, and Enis's head so full of
fans and plans, that we never seemed quite able to
center the way we used to on the thing that was
really going on between us, that awkward little
dance our two egos always did whenever they en-
countered one another.

For the most part, I stayed close to home that
year, the way an earnest newlywed grad student is
supposed to, and attended to hearth and desk. So
that when spring rolled round again, and those ogres
on my orals committee summoned me once more into
their lair, I was all primed and cocked for the occasion ("Now then, Mr. McClanahan, perhaps you
could name several, ah, female Victorian novelists
for us?" "Why yes, certainly, there was . . . *were*
. . . um, the Brontë sisters, that's three right there,
and then there was George Eliot, who was actually a
woman, as you probably know, and . . . uh . . . Jane
Eyre?"), and sweating like a piglet on a spit, I ac-
quitted myself with a performance which the chairman of the committee allowed they might consider
passable if I'd clear out of the state by sundown and
swear never to reveal to a living soul where I'd
secured my sheepskin.

In June, when I struck out for Oregon to seek my
fortune in the writing-and-teaching game, I was
sped on my way by the stiff westward wind that the

UK English Department's collective sigh of relief had given rise to.

Well, *plus ça change, plus c'est la même chose,* as they say in that Eye-talian Spanish. Get this, for instance: In the summer of 1971, when I hadn't written a printable word for months and months, when my ostensible career at the Harvard of the West had only lately perished of an anemic bibliography, and when, for all manner of other reasons there's no need, thank goodness, to go into here, my life seemed to me to be ticking away inside my breast like a time bomb planted there by some insidious cosmic assassin, at midnight on the eve of a family trip to Kentucky, intending merely to take a teensy little taste to enliven the last-minute packing of the McClanavan, I accidentally dosed myself with about two thousand micrograms of what is said to be the most stupefyingly powerful acid ever circulated around San Francisco, and spent the next twelve hours clinging like a shipwrecked sailor to the sides of my king-size California water bed, awash in my own terror, drowning all night long in the fathomless deeps of the certainty that I was going mad, dying, dead.

Now, an experience such as that will bring a man to give some serious thought to the matter of his own mortality. And as our mutual destinies would have it, mortality was also very much on Carlos Toadvine's mind just then. For on approximately the same morning that I, a survivor after all, came to among the flotsam and jetsam on that westernmost beachhead of my sanity, Enis had awakened in a Lexington hospital bed to the news that his liver would soon rival the size of his guitar, and that his next few parties would surely be his last.

(*Well, just bein' in the clubs day in and day out, why, people was just constantly sayin', "Enis, have a drank with me, buddy!" and all, and I got to where I just constantly had a drink in my hand, funnelin' it down. An arn man couldn't of stood up under what I was a-drinkin'. I would, uh, consume at least two quarts of whiskey. A day. Not countin' beer. And they was several times when I would catch myself gettin', you know, fairly drunk.*)

I didn't know that then, of course; in fact, I'd been in Lexington for weeks before the night Enis and I crossed paths again, the night when, in a fit of nameless angst, I went out driving aimlessly about town in the vain hope that the flickering pyrotechnics in my head would shed some new light on how I might go about piecing together the myriad fragments of my life and mind.

I suppose it must have been an hour or so after I'd set out that I found myself idling my motor at the Southern Railroad crossing out on South Broadway, a workingman's neighborhood of tobacco warehouses and hard-core bars and fleabag hotels and used-clothing stores, while an endless freight train oozed along before me; and after I'd sat there for several minutes, my ill-used consciousness reluc-

tantly informed me—for even a busted clock has to
tell the right time twice a day—that I was just then
situated directly across the street from the Scott
Hotel.

The Scott Hotel is a great ugly old four-story pile
of gray-green brick, with a sprinkling of quasi-
Victorian afterthoughts—turrets and gables and
oriels and cupolas—haphazardly affixed to its upper
reaches and a neon rooms-by-day-or-week sign in
the lobby window and, around the corner, a scummy
old spittoon of a tavern where, back in the days of
my callow youth, I used to go sometimes with I. J.
Wagner and Tommy Cook, to drink beer and rub
shoulders with the hoi polloi, the way any would-
Beat worthy of his whiskers was supposed to do.
The tavern, though, had evidently acquired both a
new name—Boots' Bar, according to the sign—and
a whole new entertainment policy, something rather
livelier than the six-flipper pinball machine that used
to be its main attraction; for emblazoned on the wall
facing the street, in awkwardly painted letters two
feet tall, were the words GO-GO GIRLS!

For the merest fraction of a moment, thinking
perhaps to make some sense of the future by con-
templating the ruins of my history, I considered
going in for a shot or two of Old Blast from the Past;
then, just as quickly, I thought better of it. Because
South Broadway's notion of Southern hospitality
didn't necessarily extend to loopy-looking long-hairs
in bell-bottom britches. I may be crazy—I admitted,
revving the motor—I may be crazy, but I ain't insane.

The train's caboose was in my headlights, and I had already slipped the car into gear, when I glanced back and noticed that, in three-inch letters above the GO-GO GIRLS!, with clumsy little musical notes leaping off the words like fleas leaving a sinking dog, and the letter P scrawled in by some wag with a can of spray paint, the sign said:

THE MAN WITH A GOLDEN VOICE

LITTLE ᵖENIS!

And the next thing I knew I was hooking a hard left into the Scott's parking lot . . . And the next after that, I was standing beside a blaring jukebox at the rear of a large, dark, low-ceilinged room with so much smoke in the atmosphere that I could already feel the nicotine condensing on my eyeballs, and dead ahead of me at the far end of the room was a flimsy little stage, and on the stage, bathed in pellucid greenish light, stood a lady about 156 years old, wearing green Day-Glo pasties and black bikini panties and white Easter Parade spike-heeled pumps, her bosoms a-dangle on her rib cage like two Bull Durham sacks half filled with buckshot, her stomach as scarred and dimpled as an old golf ball, her meager legs sheathed in torn nets of varicose veins, her sequin-spangled crotch thrusting fitfully to some obscure beat that she alone seemed able to discern in the strident rhythms of "Resurrection Shuffle," which is what the jukebox happened, appropriately enough, to be playing at the moment.

132

"Pour it *on*, Lucille!" someone hollered from some-where out there in the murk, and someone else hollered, "Let's see them titties fly!" And I saw that there were maybe twenty-five or thirty customers in the place, nearly all of them men, sitting in clutches of twos and threes at the tables closest to the stage, and half a dozen next-thing-to-bare-ass-nekkid ladies plying the sea of smoke with trays of drinks. I spotted an empty table over near the wall and made for it.

I needn't have worried about my hair. For I'd no sooner sat down than there emerged out of the gloom a tray-bearing damsel—she looked young enough to be Lucille's granddaughter—appareled in tasseled pasties and a sort of sequined diaper, with breasts scarcely bigger than a pair of green per-simmons and a face as amiably homely as a beagle pup's, and she walked straight up to me and put out her hand to stroke my hair and said, loudly but to no one in particular, in a voice so nasal it twanged like a broken guitar string, "Shit fahr, I wisht you'd look at the heada *hair* on hee-yim!" Then, holding my locks back with her free hand, she leaned over and planted a kiss as wet as a raw oyster smack in my left ear.

"Whatcha havin', California?" she inquired, ris-ing. Suddenly I felt like Randolph Scott, when he strides into the Barbary Coast saloon with the dust of the trail still on his boots, and the dance-hall queen sidles up to him and murmurs appreciatively, "Sa-a-a-ay! Whatcha havin', Tex?"

"Well," I said, "I guess I'll have another one of those, to start with."

"Aw, naw," she said, grinning. "One to a customer, now."

I told her I'd settle for an Oertels '92, then, if she had one. On the stage the venerable Lucille, un-resurrected but still gamely shuffling, creaked her way through the last few bars of her number, and a man's voice, hoarse with phlegm and static, issued from a two-bit loudspeaker, wheedling, "Awright, fellas, don't set on your hands, these girls'll work hard for you if you let 'em hear it." The disembodied voice paused to accommodate a listless spatter of applause, along with two or three equally half-hearted catcalls, then droned on. "That was the lovely Lucille, with skin all o-ver her bod-eh! The title of that little number was called 'It Won't Get Well If You Picket'; it's one of them good ole union songs."

"Who's that talking?" I asked the girl when she came back with my beer.

"Oh, him," she said sourly, gesturing vaguely toward the back of the room, where a seedy-looking middle-aged sport in a porkpie hat was sitting at a table by the jukebox with a glass of beer, three empty bottles, and a microphone before him. "That's Billy Bob Todd. He's supposed to be some kinda comedian."

"Well, what about Little Enis? Is he going to . . . ?"

But Billy Bob Todd was already answering my

question for me. "And now," he was saying, "here he is, the Man with a Golden Voice, and a Million Friends, Little Pee—uh, Little Enis!"

"Thank you, Billy Bird Tur—uh, Billy Bob Todd," said a familiar voice, and I looked back to the stage and there he was, perched atop a tall stool, cradling an upside-down twelve-string acoustic guitar in his arms, old Enis himself in the more than ample flesh, a rotund little bodhisattva in a polo shirt and sporty white wingtips, and slacks so snugly cut that Old Blue showed himself in bas-relief inside them, dressing left; Enis and Blue, that immortal pair, indivisible as Damon and Pythias, Abbott and Costello, Ferranté and Teicher, travelin' along singin' a song, Enis and the friend that sticketh closer than a brother.

Now there's Enis grinning impishly above his guitar to acknowledge the laugh he's won at the expense of Billy Bird Turd, Enis's tiny right hand already fingering the frets, over the top of the guitar's neck after his own heretical fashion, Enis's left hand rising involuntarily to smooth back that black-enamel hair, Enis smiling as he checks himself out in the full-length mirror mounted on the wall stage right and finds himself good, the best of all possible Enises, Enis bending to his mike to say, "Welcome to Boots' Supper Club, here in the beautiful Hotel Scott-Hilton, overlookin' the Southern Railroad tracks . . . Now here's a song I used to play when I was a boy down in Hogue Holler."

Out there in the raucous darkness I sat poised on

the edge of my seat, waiting for the opening licks of "Blue Suede Shoes" or "Rip It Up" or "Shake, Rattle, and Roll"—or even "Love Letters in the Sand"—to send me tripping off down memory lane, telling myself what a card old Enis was. Why, Enis playing "Rip It Up" in Hogue Holler would be like E. Power Biggs playing "I Took My Organ to the Party" at Carnegie Hall.

But chances are they do play "Wildwood Flower" in Hogue Holler, and that's what Enis was playing now, flat-picking little clusters of notes as sweet and delicate as periwinkles, tiny nosegays cascading down from the scratchy old loudspeaker overhead.

"How about it, California? You gonna pay me for that beer or not?"

"Oh, sorry," I said, as I dug a dollar from my pocket. "But I don't think I ever heard Enis play bluegrass before. He used to play just rock 'n' roll, mostly."

"Well," she said, "far as I'm concerned, I've done heard enough of that old hillbilly shit down home in Crab Orchard to do me for a lifetime. But Enis's been sick in the hospital, you know, he can't jump around that way no more. Hey, I bet they don't play that old hillbilly shit out there in California, do they? Shit *fahr*, I wisht I was in California and Crab Orchard, Kentucky, had a feather up its ass. Then me and it'd both be tickled."

"You better stay where you are," I told her. "These days, everybody in California talks about coming to Kentucky."

"Well," she said gloomily, "I shore do hope some of 'em comes to Crab Orchard, then."

She started to move on to the next table, but—especially since she was escaping with my change still on her tray—I figured I was entitled to another question. "Hey, Crab Orchard," I called after her, "how's Old Blue? He hasn't been sick too, has he?"

"Blue?" she said, already moving off again. "I don't know nobody by that name."

Uh oh, I thought, this could be serious. (How was it that old folksong went, the one about the hound dog? "When Old Blue died, he died so hard / He shook the ground in my back yard . . .") But Enis sure didn't *look* like a sick man, up there blithely plucking those bouquets of wildflowers off the face of his guitar like Mary, Mary, Quite Contrary. In fact, he looked perfectly fine, fat and sassy and full of vinegar, his hair still black and sleek, his eye still aglint with that old devilment, his jaw still jutting with that old bulldog audacity, a ringer for J. Edgar Hoover's renegade kid brother, the wild one that ran away to join a rock 'n' roll band twenty years ago.

And when he polished off "Wildwood Flower" and eased on into "Loose Talk" and began to sing ("When I go out walkin' / There's lots of loose talkin' . . ."), his voice seemed to me clearer and stronger and surer than ever; in the refrain ("We may have to leave here / To find peace of mind, dear . . ."), it fairly rang with the doleful, plangent tones of that chronic melancholia which, in country music, almost inevitably afflicts backstairs lovers, like a kind of psychic venereal disease.

But it was a tough house—mostly, they were there to see them titties fly—and such applause as "Loose Talk" pulled down was sparse and indifferent. Enis followed up with "Six Days on the Road," Dave Dudley's truck-driver classic, but that failed him too; this time I clapped for him almost alone, and the sound of my applause disappeared without a trace into the general hubbub of social intercourse.

"Awright now," Enis said dispiritedly, "I'm gonna play somethin' real soft this time, so I can hear you all talk."

He did an "I Kept the Wine and Threw Away the Rose" that could only have been sung by a man who'd lived it, but the trouble was that half the audience had lived it too, and evidently they weren't quite drunk enough just yet to want to be reminded of it. Then he took a shot at "Release Me," but for all his Golden Voice, Enis was no Engeldinck Humperbert, and that one didn't move them either. He filled out the set with "Sam's Place" and "Your Cheatin' Heart," and then, looking really dejected, he mumbled something about taking a break and switched off his mike.

"*Thank* you, Little Enis!" cried Billy Bob Todd. "Give him a nice hand, fellas! Enis was brought to you tonight by the makers of Black Draught. He'll be back in a little while, brought to you by the makers of Blue Ointment. But *now* . . ."

At Billy Bob's urging, they finally rewarded Enis

with a tolerably respectable little hand, and he smiled and waved and bobbed his head in the approved how-sweet-it-is fashion, like a diminutive Jackie Gleason. But when he eased himself off his stool, a sudden pain somewhere in his vitals pinched off the smile into a fleeting grimace, and I knew then that Crab Orchard's report was on the money: Little Enis, the original Glutton for Punishment, was definitely not a well man.

"But *now*, fellas," Billy Bob went on as Enis stashed his guitar and stool in the wings, "we got a very beautiful girl for you, this girl comes from a very large family—one mother and twelve fathers —here she is, the Queen of the Jungle, the lovely Edna!"

Little Richard struck up "Boney Moronie" on the jukebox, and the lovely Edna, a portly, double-chinned dumpling in a foot-tall blond bouffant wig and tasseled pasties and leopard-skin bikini bottoms, waddled onstage and began sort of marching in place to the music, phlegmatically hunching her suety loins every so often but mainly just picking up first one foot and then the other, as if she needed to go to the bathroom and had found the door locked.

"Sooo-ooo-ooeeeey!" Billy Bob hollered. Edna, sullen beneath her wig, flipped him the finger and trudged on.

The next time Crab Orchard steamed past with her tray, I flagged her down and ordered another beer. When she brought it, I asked her what it was that had put Enis in the hospital.

"I thank it was his liver," she told me, almost gaily. "They say the whiskey's just about eat it right out of him."

But she said if I wanted to talk to him during his break, I'd find him sitting in the little room beyond the bar (I looked where she was pointing in time to see Enis, his ovoid silhouette ballooning up from those pegged pants cuffs, trundle through the doorway like a toy top wobbling on its spindle), and—same old Enis—there wasn't nothing in this world, she said, that he liked better than for somebody to go back there and make over him a little.

All right, I thought when she was gone, suppose I do go back and talk to him, what then? It's bound to be another downer, I figured. First there'd be the awkward inevitabilities—"Uh, Mr. Enis, uh, you probably don't remember me, but I used to . . ."—and then we'd settle down to a leisurely, carefully considered discussion of . . . what? "The Influence of the Celtic Bardic Tradition upon the Work of Carlos Toadvine"? The fact that I'd been Doing him ("Do Enis, Ed! Do Enis!") at cocklety factail parties for nearly fifteen years now? The fact that the world was going to hell in a handbasket, and both of us were going with it?

"Looka there, fellas!" Billy Bob whooped. "Ain't that the loveliest sight you ever seen?" He was directing the beam of an oversized flashlight through the smoky dimness at the lovely Edna, Queen of the Jungle, who now stood with her back to the audience.

Little Enis: The Intimidations of Mortality

As the beam of light settled on her already almost naked backside, she reached behind her and hooked her thumbs in the waistband of her leopard-skin panties and lowered them to the tops of her thighs, the better that we might admire her opulent embarrassment of riches.

"Edna honey," Billy Bob implored, "show these boys how you can make that right one wink at 'em, now! Watch that right-hand one, boys!" Edna obligingly bunched and twitched the muscles in her right buttock, and set it to jiggling like a dish of vanilla pudding. "*Look* at that, fellas! I tell you, boys, a man could write a *book* about a thing like that!"

Well, by God, Billy Bob, a man could, at that, couldn't he? Not a book, of course, and not about Edna's ass, of course; but if a man was half a writer, he could situate old Enis in this place, this Boots' Bar where human frailty seems endlessly on parade, and do an interview or something that might—if a man was half a writer—reveal a whole hell of a lot about fame's dereliction and fate's treachery; about . . . mortality.

Sure, why not? I could go back into the past and fulfill that ancient promise; it would be a sort of second chance to set at least that one small alcove of my untidy history in order. Maybe I'd even learn something in the process, maybe he'd tell me what it was *really* like to go down for the third time and then come to and find oneself still struggling against the tide of circumstance. And right outside in the bus, buried beneath the debris of my travels, didn't I just happen to have my trusty little tape recorder? The times, they are a-wastin'!

In a trice I was outside in the McClanavan, rooting through moldy sleeping bags after my tape recorder, and in another trice I was standing over Enis's table in the back room of Boots'—where Enis sat alone and glumly pensive over a cup of Pennzoil-colored coffee—holding out the tape recorder so he couldn't miss it, saying, "Uh, Mr. Enis, uh, you probably don't remember me, but . . ." and Enis, instantly perking up and eyeing the tape recorder as thirstily as though it were a fifth of J.T.S. Brown, was saying, "An innerview, huh? You know, when I was with Jerry Lee Lewis, we was innerviewed just about ever' day, by ever' reddy-o station between here to Australia. Yeah, that guy over there was real comical, the way they talk and everthang."

And suddenly the Ed 'n' Enis Show was on the air again, Enis and I caught in our own intimate little time warp, me telling Enis how the article I intended to write about him would surely make him even richer and more famous than my master's thesis would have done; Enis telling me how he'd once been all set to get rich and famous on his own, how he'd gone on the road with Jerry Lee and played Lost Vegas with Fats Domino, how he was doing all right for himself until he came back to Lexington and the bottle brought him down (*When I was out here to the nuthouse, tryin' to get myself straightened out, they put me in this occupational therapy, you know? To occupy your mind? So they give me this big wad of clay and says, "Now, you make whatever's on your mind, Enis." So I made me a little canoe, see, and a little Indian a-layin' in it. Not doin' nothing, just a-layin' there! And painted it blue! The whole thing, boat and Indian and all! And that shrinker says to me, "Now, Enis, what do you reckon that* stands *for?" And I says, "Why, it looks to me like that's just what was occupyin' my mind! Nothin'! Not one damn thing! I reckon I'm just like that old Indian!"*), and how . . .

Along about here on the tape is where the lovely Edna, carrying an empty tray in one hand and cupping the right side of her jaw in the other, comes slouching in and sinks into a chair and moans, "Aaaaah shit, I *can't* wait no more goddamn tables, I got a goddamn abscess tooth! *Plus* it's my goddamn period. Lemme hide out back here with you all for a minute."

Out front somebody is indifferently plucking at a guitar. I tilt my chair back to where I can look through the door into the other room. Billy Bob Todd has mounted the stage and is sitting on Enis's stool, with Enis's guitar across his lap. He is getting about as much music from it as Enis would from flat-picking a barbed-wire fence.

"That son-of-a-bitch Billy Bob is gonna get my guitar outta tune again," Enis grumps. "He thinks he's a picker. Sheeit. He couldn't pick his mother out of a spastic parade."

Edna, gingerly probing along her gum line with

a grubby forefinger, notices the tape recorder mike at her elbow. "What're you all doin'?" she snickers around her finger. "Broadcastin' to outer space?"

(Well, *hidy*, out there in the void, friends and neighbors! This here's your Ed 'n' Enis Show, where all the action's at! We got it all right here, we got crude dudes and lewd nudes, we got Ed and Enis and Edna's Ass, we got Old Blue and Billy Bird Turd, we got Twenty Girls Twenty, we got . . .)

"This boy here," Enis is telling Edna, setting her straight, "this boy here is Ned McManahan, he's a p'fessor at a colletch. He's fixing to write a book on my life story."

We got, like I said, the same old Enis. But Edna coolly appraises me and is plainly not impressed. "This nerve is dying," she declares as her finger disappears into her mouth again. "The gobgamn nerve is dying."

And how (Enis went on) this last time the high life had almost laid him low for keeps. *Well, we was playin' out here to Comer's Bar, and I just keeled over, right there on the stage, and never woke up till eight days later. And when I come out of my coma, that doctor told me that if I was to start in drinkin' again, I wouldn't live a good two weeks. See, they had went up in me with a tube and tuck a picture of my liver, and it was just a-floatin' in there! So what I mean, I cannot consume no amount of alcoholic beverages whatsoever, hardly. 'Cause you just as well start talkin' to the Good Man Upstairs when your liver goes out on you.*

144

Little Enis: The Intimidations of Mortality

I heard the click inside the tape recorder that told me we were out of tape, which was just as well, because a moment later Crab Orchard came in to remind Enis that it was almost midnight, time for his last set.

"Hey, Enis," I said, "Crab Orchard here tells me she's never been introduced to Old Blue! How'd you let that happen?"

Despite the miseries in her tooth, the lovely Edna managed a knowing smile at the memory of Old Blue. But Enis took my remark at face value and answered the question accordingly.

"Well," he said gravely, "your liver, see, controls all the har-mone cells in your body. And after I come out of that hospital, I just didn't have no har-mones left, hardly. But they been givin' me these shots, and they say it won't be long now till . . ." Noticing Crab Orchard standing over him looking characteristically perplexed, Enis grinned and patted her naked haunch. "Aw yeah, Crab Apple, honey, you'd like Old Blue, if you just knowed him. He's got a head like a housecat, and ribs like a hungry hound."

This time Crab Orchard got it. She giggled and slapped lightly at Enis's hand and said, Why-Enis-you-awful-thang-you, but she didn't really mean it. She even blushed a little, as if something within her recognized that his very lubricity bespoke a crazy kind of boyish innocence, that after his own fashion he was being a perfect gentleman, he was being *courtly*. Old Blue was his Excalibur, and Enis had presented him to her even as the gallants of King

Arthur's court must have offered up their swords in service to their ladies.

"Listen here, you dirty man," Crab Orchard said, "if you're so hot to trot, whyn't you go out there and play me some rock 'n' roll? I'm *tard* of that ol' country shit."

"Hey, yeah!" I put in. "Do some Jerry Lee Lewis songs! Do Elvis!"

"Oh lordy," Enis said, wincing as he struggled to his feet, "I don't know, I got awful bad water on the knee tonight, I don't know if I can . . ."

He'd do it, though, I realized as I watched him go gamely hobbling off after Crab Orchard: he'd do it because there was a show happening in his head too, a one-man spectacular starring Carlos Toadvine as the Incomparable Enis, and *that* show must go on, water on the knee or not. He'd do it because he was a trouper, a real little trouper. And besides, if Carlos Toadvine missed a performance, who else could play the role?

"Sounds like Old Blue's been under the weather too," I said to Edna as I gathered up my gear to move back into the other room.

Edna favored me with yet another smile, a wistful one this time. "Aww, that Enis," she mused fondly, a faraway look in her eye. "He sure used to be somethin', he sure did." I started to ask her if she'd care to make a statement to that effect for publication, but just then a sudden twinge in her tooth brought that wet slug of a finger back into her mouth, so I reconsidered and went on out.

By the time I'd picked up a beer at the bar and found myself a table, Enis was onstage, perched on his stool retuning his guitar after Billy Bob's irreverent trifling. His melancholia had evidently passed; he was grinning, and that old roguish gleam was in his eye, that incorrigible vintage-Enis cheekiness which, inscribed upon this roly-poly latter-day Enis's chubby little features, put me in mind of a concupiscent choirboy, a randy cherub. Right then it wouldn't have surprised me in the least if Old Blue himself had come dancing out on Enis's knee, spiffy as Mr. Peanut, with a little top hat and a monocle and maybe a little white wing-tip collar and a walking stick, Stage-Door Johnny Blue doing a sprightly buck-and-wing to the tune of "Fit as a Fiddle," Old Blue in the pink again, fit as a fiddle and ready for love. Somehow I was already beginning to suspect that this set just might turn out to be an altogether different story from the last one.

"The girls'll be back in a minute, fellas," Billy Bob advised us. "They're shaving, right now. But here's the man you've all been waiting for, the Man with a Golden Voice, the one and only, the *fabulous* Little Enis!"

A pit-a-pat of applause greeted the announcement, but the audience was still restive, still a good deal more taken up with its own concerns—ordering another round, going out to take a leak, grab-assing the waitresses—than it was with whatever Enis had to offer. This time, though, Enis was up to the challenge; he was eyeing his indifferent audience as cockily as the lecherous pissant in that old joke, the one who crawls up an elephant's leg with seduction on his mind.

But the first order of business is to get the elephant's attention. "Now, here's a nice little song," Enis said, "if you like nasty dirty old songs." He picked off a tantalizingly swift run of warm-up notes, then added, "But this song ain't really dirty. It's just all dependin' where your mind is at.

> *Any ice today, ladies?*
> *Any ice today, ladies?*
> *How about a little piece today?"*

That did it; as the song went on ("There's a lady lives on Ninth Street, / Her name is Missuz Brown; / She takes ice most ev'ry day, / Got the biggest box in town"), it got ranker ("There's a lady lives on Tenth Street, / Her name is Missuz Green; / She don't get no ice today, / 'Cause her damned ol' box ain't clean") and ranker ("I'm a very nice iceman, / I won't cheat you, of course; / But if you want a bigger piece, / I'll have to get my horse"), and the ranker the song became, the more clamorously the crowd acclaimed it; it woke them up and broke them up, jacked them up and cracked them up; they cheered and clapped and stomped and whistled so lustily that by the end of the last verse ("I'm a very nice iceman, / That's very plain to see; / But hurry up and put it in, / It's drippin' . . . on . . . m' knee!"), the din of their enthusiasm nearly drowned out the final chorus.

"Aw yeah," Enis said as soon as they'd settled back a bit, "I'm a go-getter. My wife works, and I go get 'er!" With that he launched into a "Salty Dog" as spiritedly priapic as a sailor home on shore leave; and in the little theater inside my head Old Blue danced onstage again, an amorous old salt in navy bell-bottoms and a tiny white swabbie cap cocked low and rakish on his beetled brow, like Gene Kelly in *Anchors Aweigh.* As Blue took his bow and cake-walked off into the wings, Enis stopped a go-go lady who was just then passing before the stage—a hefty, hulking, heavy-breasted girl in a wig like a double-dip cone of Dairy Whip—and said, "Hey, Big 'Un, honey, would you brang me a Co-Cola? Maybe I can *drownd* this goddamn liver." While she shambled off to fetch the Coke, he killed time with a few more bars of "Salty Dog," just idling his motor, letting us know he wasn't finished with us yet, not by a long shot. When the Big 'Un came back with his glass of Coke, he tossed the whole thing off in one long swallow, and wiped his mouth with the back of his hand.

"Now then, sweetheart," he said, pointing the bottom of the glass at her orange-tasseled natural endowments, "let's me and you show these boys how you can start them things by hand on a cold mornin'."

The Big 'Un, recognizing her cue, nodded happily and set down her tray and turned to face the audience, and Enis said, "Now, here's a little number I learnt when I was on the road with Jerry Lee Lewis," and laced into "Great Balls of Fire," and the

Big 'Un, bouncing in double-time on her toes, grabbed herself a handful of her left breast, gave it a fierce counterclockwise flip, and set its tassel to spinning, slowly and erratically at first, like the prop on Jimmy Stewart's plane in one of those old You-can't-send-the-kid-up-in-a-crate-like-that movies, then faster and faster as she warmed up, as *Enis* warmed up— "*Hook* it, Enis!" somebody hollered. "*Hook* it, son!" —and then she laid hold of her right breast and cranked it up the way she had the other one, clockwise this time, she was a DC-3 revving up on the runway, her prop wash swirled the smoke about her, and now Enis was really digging in, getting after it—"Y' shake m' nerves and y' rattle m' brain, / Too much *luhhhv* / Drives a man insane!"—the All-American Left-Handed Upside-down Guitar Player had his chops back, for now at least; that big twelve-string rang out as though Jerry Lee himself had crawled inside it, Jerry Lee and a concert grand and the entire New York Philharmonic Orchestra—"Y' broke m' will, / But what a *threee*-ill!"—the *Enis Hour* was on the air, brought to you in living Enis-color through the miracle of Enisvision, featuring the interpretive dance stylings of the lovely Big 'Un and the noted impressionist Old Blue, and starring the Enis the World Awaited, the Man with a Golden Voice and a Million Friends, the Man with . . .

Good-*nis* gray-*shus*, gret *balls o' fie-yer!*

But how about that curious-looking long-haired party out there in the audience, the one in the Cali-

fornia getup, the one with his fortieth birthday
hard upon him and his mind blown as full of holes
as Enis's liver, the one who's leaping half out of
his chair, hollering, "Do Elvis, Enis! Do 'All Shook
Up'! Do 'Hound Dog'! Do 'Lawdy Miss Clawdy'!
Do . . ."?

Uh huh; me again. The old Loose End again, the
Noted Arthur again, stoned again. The more things
change, the more they stay the same, and here
comes another one, just like the other one. Because
suddenly Enis was down off that stool and on his
feet, and his left knee—water and all—was pumping
inside his pants as though he wore a jackhammer
for a peg leg with a hot-water bottle for a kneepad,
and he was seesawing his guitar back and forth
across the swell of his belly and cranking away at
the face of it like a demented organ grinder, singing,
"Well, bless-a mah soul, whuzz-a wrong wi' me? /
Ah'm a-eetchin' lak a bug on a fuzzeh tree," and the
Big 'Un was about to take off into the wild blue
yonder, and I was belaboring my tabletop with all
my old abandon—like Enis, at least for now I had
my chops back—everything had slipped back into
sync, I could *recognize* myself again; I mean, I'd
know that guy anywhere, no matter what disguise
he wore, that's just old Fred Callahan, the noted
Enisologist from out at the colletch, he's been trying
to find his way back to this moment for nearly
fifteen years, and now at last he's here; he and Enis
and Old Blue too, they're a little the worse for the
wear, maybe, but they've all made it this far more

or less intact, Old Blue can still rise to the occasion when he gets his booster shots, and the Enis That Shook the World can shake it still, and their accompanist Jed McMickelhan, the old California mutant, is still the premiere tabletop percussionist in all of Rockabillydom, just *listen* at 'em wail, just listen at that "Lawdy Miss Clawdy," that "Hi-yo, Silver," that "Hound Dog," that "Kansas City," that "Blue Suede Shoes"; why, these boys coulda been *stars* if they'd just kept that act together: Enis would be on the cover of *Rolling Stone, Playboy* would run a full-color spread of Lucille and Crab Orchard and Edna and the Big 'Un and all the Enisettes, *The New Yorker* would do a four-part profile of Old Blue, *Psychology Today* would editorialize on the phenomenon of Enis envy in American culture, and Professor TedNedFredJed McHammerclan would deliver a brilliant lecture entitled "The Influence of the Celtic Bardic Tradition upon the Work of Carlos Toadvine" at the Juilliard Colletch of Musical Knowletch; they coulda made it big, they coulda played Carnegie Hall, they coulda been, by God, *immortal*!

Ah, but what voice is this I hear, croaking down at me across the years from the pedagogical summit I so long ago aspired to? "Now then, Mr. McClanahan, in his 'Ode on Intimations of Immortality,' Wordsworth asks himself the rhetorical question 'Whither is fled the visionary gleam? / Where is it now, the glory and the dream?' Perhaps you could tell us—*pull yourself together, man!*—how the poet, in his maturity, consoles himself in the poem's closing quatrain for the loss of that youthful vision of immortality?"

Why, certainly, Dr. Earwigg (I might've answered if I hadn't skipped out on all those seminars), I do believe the lines in question are, if memory serves, the following:

> *Thanks to the human heart by which we live,*
> *Thanks to its tenderness, its joys, and fears,*
> *To me the meanest flower that blows can give*
> *Thoughts that do often lie too deep for tears.*

SEVEN

Drowning in the Land of Sky-Blue Waters

One used-car salesman to another in
the Elbow Room Bar in Missoula,
Montana: *"Who made the most money
last year? I did, by God! So don't tell
me you're the goddamn epitome of
virtue!"*

THIS all begins about where it will end, way up in the upper-left-hand corner of the country, where I am lumbering along a Montana freeway in a cumbersome, sway-backed old white whale of a '65 Chevy van named Moldy Dick, headed east, into the very first sunrise of July 1976. At my back is a U-Haul trailer and, receding into both the distance and the past, the town of Missoula, Montana, which until this morning I've called home for all of three years now. Ahead of Moldy Dick and me is my new bride Cia, piloting the ageless, long-suffering McClanavan, and ahead of her are a couple of thousand miles of eastbound highway, at the far end of which is a tumbledown, four-room tenant house on a high bank of the Kentucky River, near the hamlet of Port Royal, in Henry County, Kentucky. In Moldy and the U-Haul are two-thirds of all our worldly possessions; in the VW, with Cia, is the other third. We have no money to speak of, no jobs, no prospects. Yet, as must ever be the case with nearly-newlyweds, our hopes are high. We are nesters, homesteaders, a weird little wagon train in the Eastward Movement, pioneers seeking our earthly paradise.

This is not the first time Cia and I have hit this trail in hot pursuit of the wild goose. Exactly ten months ago to the very day—on September 1, 1975—we set out from Missoula on this same highway, in the same direction, with the same destination—but that time it took seven weeks and seven thousand miles to get there, and another seven weeks and seven thousand miles to get back, and along the way we drank enough beer to drown the entire feline population of Ardmore, Oklahoma. There'll be no such dawdling on this trip; we're humping to make it to Kentucky in time to get a very late garden in the ground, so we'll at least have a few turnips to gnaw on this coming winter. But that other trip, that was a hoot, buddies. It liked to kilt us.

I still don't know for sure whose idea it was, but it seemed like a winner at the time. There we were in Missoula in the spring of '75, Cia working in the public library and I rounding out my second, and last, year as a utility factotum in the University of Montana's creative-writing program, my career as a professional Visiting Lecturer finally about to come a cropper, apparently for good. I was still pecking desultorily away at my poor old dead letter of a novel, and Cia was writing songs and short stories during her coffee breaks at the library, but neither of us had much heart for the business. Like everyone else in Missoula—where the outdoors closes up shop in November and doesn't reopen till around the summer solstice—we spent most of our free time in the bars, soaking our anxieties in Dutch courage and cowboy blues.

And then one fateful night, probably at the AmVets Club, where there was a fine country house band and a nice little dance floor, upon which Cia had long endeavored, with indifferent success, to improve my elephantine impression of the Texas two-step, one or the other of us—I'll take the blame —was struck by a stray bolt of lightning from a passing brainstorm.

"Hey, do you realize we could make a *living* doing this?"

"What, dancing? Are you out of your mind?"

"No no, I mean we could hang out in places like this and *write* about them!"

"About honky-tonks!"

"Honky-tonks, dives, juke joints—!"

"About country music!"

"We could write a *book*!"

"Yeah! We could travel around, goin' to honky-tonks, and write a *book* about it!"

"Hey, yeah! We could get a *contract*, we could . . ."

Something like that. By the time Cia got her feet out from under mine, we'd two-stepped our way into a whole new cottage industry. Within the next few weeks, with the help of several rather credulous Friends in High Places, we snagged a small option from a New York publisher, along with, more important, a letter of introduction certifying that we were accredited knights of the plume and ought to be extended every courtesy. Our plan was to stay in Missoula through the coming summer, outfitting the McClanavan for camping and getting into drinking shape for the long haul, and then to hit the road in September for a couple of months, in the general direction of Kentucky, my home turf, where we'd sit out the winter. Then we'd honky-tonk it back to Missoula in the spring, arriving triumphant with our manuscript in hand and our Pulitzer Prize virtually a foregone conclusion. *Saturday Night*, we'd call the book; *Saturday Night: Honky-tonkin' in Hard Times.* Perfect!

Well, maybe not quite perfect. For one thing, we dreamed up this terrific title in 1975, about fifteen minutes before *Saturday Night Live* hit the TV and *Saturday Night Fever* hit the screen and the Bay City Rollers' "Saturday Night" hit the pop charts and Tom Waits's "The Heart of Saturday Night" hit the album charts. So our timing wasn't all that hot. And just how *do* two people write a book together? Don't ask us, because we never got ours written.

Not that it matters, since it was clearly a book the world could get along without, as the world has subsequently demonstrated, to a nicety. But we did make the trip; we actually put in all that time and all those miles jukin' and jivin' and juicin' our way through hundreds—hundreds!—of bars, dancehalls, roadhouses, juke joints, and "low drinking resorts" (which is what my dictionary calls honky-tonks), earnestly interviewing every musician, barkeep, and barfly we could corner, researching the definitive study in downward mobility, looking, as Tom Waits has it, for the heart of Saturday night.

And we found it. I am pleased to announce, here and now, that the Quintessential Pluperfect Para-

mount Honky-tonk of the Known World is the Town
Tavern in Osgood, Indiana—or anyhow it *was*, one
Saturday night in December 1975.

Honky-tonking, see, is like stalking the Loch Ness
monster; what counts are the sightings, not bringing
home the varmint's gory fleece. The quarry is at
once as ubiquitous as Santa Claus and as elusive as
a snipe; scarcely a citizen of the realm is more than
twenty-five miles or so from a honky-tonk experience
of the highest order on any given Saturday night
(or almost any other night of the week, for that
matter), yet even the most dogged and enterprising
roisterers are assured of no reward save a repentant
Sunday morning for their efforts, if luck and intui-
tion aren't with them.

The night before we went to Osgood, for instance,
at a popular country nitespot in Louisville, a pall
of boredom as palpable as cigarette smoke hung all
evening long over a crowd of some three hundred
dispirited revelers (ourselves among them), despite
the best efforts of a tight, hardworking house band
and the usually enlivening presence of several apparently unattached charmers in high heels and hot
pants. Whereas, the very next night up in Osgood,
it required only some fifteen celebrants (our vagrant
selves again among them) and two road-weary old
guitar-pickers named Singin' Sam and Ramblin' Joe
to raise the Town Tavern's roof nigh unto outtasight.

In fact, we eventually concluded, all that's really
required for the primary honky-tonk alchemy to

work is a good country jukebox and a solitary beer
drinker. Imagine, for example, some poor old homesick hillbilly sitting all alone in a Detroit briarhopper beer joint at closing time, plugging the
jukebox with his last quarter for one—no, *two!*—
more plays of Bobby Bare's great citybilly blues
song "Detroit City"—which is *about* him!—and
you're as close to the fundamental implosion as it's
safe to stand, probably. The honky-tonk is the cru-
cible in which this phenomenon occurs, when artist
and audience are fused in the commonality of their
experience.

You can't make a sow's ear out of a silk purse,
of course; Charlie Rich doth not of Caesar's Palace
a honky-tonk make. But when Johnny Allen and
the Memories lay into "Jolie Blonde" in BooBoo's
Niteclub in Breaux Bridge, Louisiana, and four
hundred exultant Cajuns storm the dance floor . . .
when the All-American Left-Handed Upside-down
Guitar Player keens "I Kept the Wine and Threw
Away the Rose" to his audience of redneck dead-
beats in some Lexington, Kentucky, dive, exhorting
them—too late, alas, too late!—to beware the perils
of ambition, the blandishments of bright lights and
city ways . . . when Bobby Bare's morose beer
drinker communes with himself and his sources ("I
wanna go home . . . Ohh, how I wanna go home!")
through the medium of the jukebox . . . that's a
honky-tonk, dearly beloved, that's a holy place!

Not to make too much of this holiness business,
though; there's really nothing all that sanctified

about establishments that treat so openly with the Devil.* You can get hurt in a thousand ways in a honky-tonk: you can break your heart, ruin your health, lose your religion, and get your ass handed to you; virtuous women are metamorphosed overnight into tramps, strong men are reduced to— in the parlance—knee-walkin', commode-huggin' drunks; lovers murder one another in honky-tonks; if you're the passive type, you can simply, quietly drown in beer, bad music, and other people's bullshit in a honky-tonk.

And the undertow, I'm here to tell you, is something fierce.

The fact is, we didn't know ourselves what we were getting into when we undertook this endeavor. Oh, we'd honked and tonked around some in our time, and country music had long been among our mutual abiding passions—but we certainly never reckoned with the honky-tonk blues.

The honky-tonk blues is a malady brought on by

---

* Honky-tonk music itself testifies endlessly and eloquently to the general unwholesomeness of its own environs: to genial, joyless alcoholism ("Pop-A-Top," "What Made Milwaukee Famous [Has Made a Loser Out of Me]," "Wine Me Up," "Little Ole Winedrinker—Me," etc., etc., etc.), to aimless sexuality ("From Barrooms to Bedrooms"), to marital restlessness ("The Wild Side of Life"), to the failure of religious faith ("The Lord Knows I'm Drinkin' "), to violent political resentments ("The Fightin' Side of Me"), even to the insalubrity of the very atmosphere ("Smoky the Bar").

overexposure to the wild side of life. People who frequent low drinking resorts eight nights a week are liable to get—vulgarity says it best—they get *fucked up*. They are assaulted by too much truth and, at the same time, too many lies; they lose their sense of proportion, of balance; their vision of reality is chronically blurred by alcohol and elation and hangover and depression, they get manic, they are by turns garrulous and quarrelsome, their dispositions sour, they fight among themselves over imagined slights and shadowy suspicions; in the dark of their minds they brood upon mortality and, worse, upon the death of love. A dreadful affliction, all in all—and one to which writers have no more natural immunity than the veriest illiterate.

Yet from Alberton, Montana, to Breaux Bridge, Louisiana, to Osgood, Indiana . . . and back again . . . we pursued our evanescent quarry, through trials and travails, despite pitfalls and pratfalls, following our noses and our muses and, sometimes, our muses' noses, sticking whenever possible to the back roads and small towns, a hundred, two hundred miles a day, camping or putting up in out-of-the-way cheap motels, barhopping like Hav-A-Hank salesmen, nine or ten noisy, noisome clubs a night sometimes, starting conversations, relentlessly ingratiating ourselves, asking questions, swilling toxic fluids and breathing noxious fumes, taking endless notes that regularly progressed, in the course of an evening, from lucid to addled to delirious to indecipherable, but that always included a smattering of hot tips for the next town down the road (*Rhonda waitress at Paree Lounge in Baton Rouge sez don't miss MaryJane's in Baytown, Tex., that's where they do the Goat-roper . . .*), clarion calls to duty that kept us pressing ever onward.

It was just such a hot tip that led us to Singin' Sam and Ramblin' Joe at the Town Tavern, up in Osgood. We'd driven nearly sixty miles to find it, on the recommendation of a bartender in a place called, I swear, the M&M Disco & Bait Shop in Carrollton, Kentucky. At first blush the Town Tavern didn't look much more promising than the M&M had proved. Although it was the very shank of a Saturday evening, there were scarcely a dozen folks on hand, and most of them looked sullen and mopish, as if the two grizzled old minstrels cranking out "Waltz Across Texas" on the bandstand were keeping them awake. A couple of fat ladies were essaying a sort of ponderous mazurka on a dance floor the size of a double bed, but otherwise the Town Tavern's vital signs were pretty feeble.

Then, wonder of wonders, while we were still settling in at our table, the bartender came over to tell us that we'd just won the door prize—a case of Schlitz! How about *that*, we exulted, let's set up the house! An inspired move, for it instantly won us a dozen new friends at no cost whatsoever to ourselves, inasmuch as the new friends were simultaneously obliged to set *us* up before the night was over. Within minutes people were drinking our health and smiling upon us from every corner of

the room; Sam 'n' Joe saluted us from the bandstand
and picked up the tempo, a couple of skinny old boys
got up to join the fat ladies on the dance floor, and
in short order the joint was jumpin' like a hatful of
grasshoppers. We were the life the party had been
waiting for. I danced with all the ladies, Cia danced
with all the gents, and after we'd discreetly put
out the word that we were writers, they all wanted
to buy us even more beer and tell us their life stories.
Sam and Joe took their breaks at our table and told
us *their* life stories ("So I had me a job all lined up
with Bill Monroe and the Blue Grass Boys, and
that's when I mashed my hand in my cousin Randy's
trailer hitch . . ."), and then Sam's wife, Irene,
showed up and told us *her* life story ("Yeah, him and
me met at the Old Dominion Theater, in Alexandria,
Virginia . . ."). Sometime late in the proceedings,
Joe mentioned that his real name was Howard
Miceburger. Well then, I inquired, how come he
called himself Ramblin' Joe? "We-e-e-el," he allowed
thoughtfully, "I couldn't hardly call myself Ramblin'
Howard Miceburger, I reckon." At closing time, the
bartender gave us two free six-packs for the road—
and told us his life story.

Neon lights, midnight madness:

In Butte, Montana, after we'd tripped the light
fantastic for hours at the Helsinki Baths Bar &
Grill to the lilting cacophanies of Frankie Yankovic's
brother Johnny's polka band, we fell into a place
called Dirty-Mouth Jean's for a nightcap, and the
well-dressed matron behind the bar took Cia's order,

then turned to me and said, "And what'll this prick have?"

In Clovis, New Mexico, at the Cellar Bar in the basement of the Hotel Clovis, I danced with a lady whose earrings featured her late husband's gallstones.

In Luke's Cool Spot in Carrollton, Kentucky, the bartender, a former professional wrestler named Oscar the Mountain Ox, whiled away his idle moments squashing cockroaches on the bar with the bottom of a beer bottle.

In the Wonder Bar in Walsenburg, Colorado, of all places, we ran into a melancholy young drunk named Steve, who told us he was the son of a great American athlete, an Olympic distance runner so famous that I instantly recognized the name. "I love to drink, get drunk," Steve acknowledged gloomily. "I'm angry, bitter, vitriolic. And all because of . . . track."

In the Starlite Eats & Beer, on a back road somewhere in eastern Arkansas, the woebegone old soak sitting next to me at the bar, who was drinking beer and simultaneously gumming an immense chew of tobacco, decided that introductions were in order. "M' name," he announced, in a voice as thick and damp as pond slime, "is Rrrrrraymon' Mmmmmmurphy. Rrrrrraymon' is m' firs' name. An' Mmmmmmurphy is m' las' name." "Don't pay no attention to Raymond," interjected the bartender, swatting a fly on the back bar. "He's like these damn flies. He eats shit and bothers people."

Famous People I Have Known

In the parking lot behind Tex's Barrelhouse, in Bakersfield, California, we saw a cowboy sitting on the running board of an old pickup truck, fastidiously throwing up into his boot.

In the back streets of Houston late one sweltering Sunday night, we landed in a mosquito-infested open-air beer joint called Kountry Korners, where a hulking truck driver named Leon was striving mightily, though to little avail, to pass his fleshy, thirty-eight-year-old person off as a reincarnation of Elvis Presley, c. 1957. Leon had the requisite guitar, pompadour, sideburns, and repertoire, but he was sadly lacking in the talent department. He worked hard at it, though—grinding out what seemed an endless medley of old Elvis rockers and sweating like a one-man Texas chain gang—and his enthusiasm was worth a lot all by itself. At his break I bought him a beer, and asked if he'd care to sum up his life story in a few well-chosen words. "Aw," Leon said, mopping his greasy brow, "I've played 'em all, from the biggest to the littlest. My biggest was a soul gig in a thirty-six-lane bowlin' alley, had a twelve-piece band and three colored girls behind me. Ever' poor boy's got the same dream, see, the same damn dream: set his mother up in a nice place."

In the only bar in Kooskia, Idaho, the barmaid pointed to her feet and said, "See these sandals? Day before yesterday, they was boots. That's what happens when you dance all weekend."

In a Holiday Inn cocktail lounge on the Interstate archipelago somewhere in the vicinity of Atlanta, I asked the solitary drinker at the bar whether he happened to know of any live music in the area. "Naw," he said, "all I know is how to get back on the Interstate. I never been in Tennessee before."

In the Chicken Ranch in Austin, at the break, the bandleader stepped to the mike and said, "Now, you all get you a beer, and be thankful that you drink. If you didn't drink, when you wake up in the morning, that's as good as you'd feel all day."

And in the M&M Disco & Bait Shop, a hairy, leathery little backwoods hippie, who called himself Pisswilliger and looked like a three-day-old road-kill, told us he'd just finished pulling two years in the state pen. Too polite to ask what he'd been in for, we inquired instead what he intended to do, now that he was out. *"Do?"* he cried indignantly. "I ain't gonna do nothing, by God! They wouldn't let me do what I wanna do, so I just ain't gonna do nothing, by God!" Well, we asked, what was it you wanted to do, Pisswilliger? "Why," he fumed, "I *wanted* to sell pot and pills to the high school kids, by God!"

And so, on. And so, forth.

Now don't get me wrong, we went to uptown places too, and we heard some wonderful music and met some lovely folks. We swang and swayed to the sweetest house band in the land—that'd be the nameless "bunch of Merle Haggard rejects" (their description) at J.D.'s Cocktail Lounge in Ridgecrest, California—we heard Pretty Jan Dell at the Cabin in Milltown, Montana, and the Salt Creek Boys at Ziggy's in New Orleans and the Juice

Commanders at the Club Imperial in Vicco, Kentucky, and Curly Cook at the Caravan East in Albuquerque and Lonny Mitchell's Zydeco Band at Mitchell's Lounge in Houston and Oscar Whittington at the Democrat Hot Springs Inn in Democrat Hot Springs, California, and the White Trash Liberation Front at Mac's Bar in Thermopolis, Wyoming, and Doug Sahm at the Soap Creek Saloon in Austin and Asleep at the Wheel at the Palomino in L.A.; we followed the great Clifton Chenier and His Red-Hot Louisiana Band from Antone's in Austin to the Bamboo Lounge in Rayne, Louisiana, to Boo-Boo's in Breaux Bridge; we ate steak at the Lowake Inn in Lowake, Texas, and crawfish at Elmer Naquin's Crawfish Kitchen in Breaux Bridge, and tacos and beans at La Fiesta in Clovis, New Mexico, and hot boudin sausages at Mitchell's Lounge and cheeseburgers at the Broken Drum Café ("You Can't Beat It!") in Hayden, Colorado, and catfish (nobody's gonna believe this, but it's true all the same) at the LBJ Ranch; we drank more beer than the Pittsburgh Steelers and danced more miles than Arthur Murray and listened to more life stories than Sigmund Freud.

During our midwinter layover in Kentucky, we holed up in this abandoned tenant house beside the Kentucky River, just down the road from our old friends Wendell and Tanya Berry. The little house was in a bad way, but then so were we by that time; after all those days and nights in that VW, it seemed extravagantly well appointed, and as roomy as all outdoors. And the location was just grand—a pretty river at our doorstep, a garden on the riverbank, a CinemaScope view of the valley without another house in sight. It was the perfect setup for a pair of old nearly-newlyweds. As soon as we got our land legs back, we began to see that this place was definitely going to figure in our future, if we could only manage to outlive the present.

At Christmas time we went to Lexington to pay a sick call on my irrepressible old pal Little Enis, who was in a bad way too. He had what he called "sclerosis of the liver," his kidneys were failing, his heart was beating as erratically as a one-legged drummer in a marching band, varicose veins as thick as grapevines looped his poor skinny little legs, clots the size of goose eggs coursed his bloodstream. Seeing him, I was reminded that a linguist friend of mine once suggested that "Toda-vinney" probably used to mean "all the wine." But Enis had just one regret. "I shoulda been a preacher," he declared intrepidly. "I like fried chicken and pussy as well as anybody."

Enis died February 27, 1976. We were in Austin, working west, when the word came. I sent flowers, and a card that said "So long, little buddy." Then I sat in the McClanavan and cried like a baby, in the terrible knowledge that the more things stay the same, the more they change, and not even immortality lasts forever.

This whole ramble was beginning to get to us. We'd bottomed out resoundingly in Baton Rouge one night the week before, bombing along from the Kozy Keg to the Club Riviera to Silvio's Grille to the Paree Lounge to the Sugar Patch to the Silver Dollar Café to the Twilight Lounge to an oblivion so profound that neither of us has ever been able to recall where we went next. Call it the Dew Drop Inn; in a town the size of Baton Rouge, there's bound to be a Dew Drop Inn. We don't remember either exactly what occasioned our little disagreement in the parking lot as we were leaving; but we must have administered each other a pretty thorough going-over, because our bruised feelings didn't recover for days and days. This was no way to run a honeymoon, I'll tell you that.

And it kept on happening; we high-centered again, more or less similarly, in Nederland, Texas, in Tiny Richardson's Club 88, and again in El Paso at the Maverick Club, and again in Albuquerque at the Thunderbird, and again in Yuma at Johnny's Other Place, and again in Bakersfield at the Silver Spur, and again in Redding at the Oak Grove Club . . .

A chronic case of the honky-tonk blues, compounded by a touch of motion sickness; the wild side of life had just about undone us. Too much beer and bad music and bullshit—our own as well as other people's—too many renditions of "Proud Mary" by too many groups with names like the Soporifics or Randy Snopes and the New Country Moods, too many hangovers, too many fights in the parking lots of too many Dew Drop Inns. As the old Jim

Reeves song says, we'd enjoyed as much of this as we could stand.

By the time we limped back into Missoula in early April of '76, we understood all too well that if our collaboration had a future, it had better be in babies, not in books. But our travels weren't over yet, for we already had our sights set on that sweet little house back there on the bank of the Kentucky, where a couple of newly minted homebodies like us could settle in and get down to some serious collaborating.

So here we are just three months later, heading east—only it isn't July the first anymore, it's July the seventh, and we've spent the past four days in Sheridan, Wyoming, high-centered once again. It wasn't our fault this time, though; we've been waiting for Sheridan's inevitable hippie VW mechanic to repair the McClanavan, after the depredations lately visited upon it by Missoula's hippie VW mechanic, the most recent of a legion of that irksome ilk.

Sheridan turned out to be a nice town, with a lovely cheap motel and two or three of the bulliest cowboy bars we found anywhere; and it was fine to make the rounds without questions to ask, notes to take, books to write. Anxious as we've been to get on the move, we've had a good time there, one last little blast before we hit that turnip patch.

Now we're back on the road, Cia still leading in

the McClanavan, Moldy and I and the U-Haul bringing up the rear. For the first fifty miles or so out of
Sheridan, I've tailed her pretty close, expecting her
poor old spavined steed to start spewing oil all over
the roadway at any moment, like it did four days
ago.

But everything seems to be in good order this
morning, so finally I relax my vigil and fall back a
ways. These old bangers of ours cruise at about
forty-five, flat out, which makes for a long, lazy day
at the wheel. Any other time, lollygagging along all
by myself like this, I'd sit back, pop the top of a
cold Grain Belt, and tune in the nearest call-in show
on the radio. There's a problem, though: Moldy Dick,
which we bought for four hundred bucks just for
this trip, came with a gaping hole, like a missing
tooth, in the dash where the radio should have been.
So, left to my own devices, too uncoordinated to
twiddle my thumbs and steer at the same time, I'm
casting about for something to occupy the vasty
fastnesses of my mind for the next few hundred
miles. And that's when I remember the Elbow
Room, and the Born in the Land of Sky-Blue Waters
sign.

The Elbow Room is a nondescript bar in a nondescript building which squats nondescriptly amid
the used-car-lot ghetto on the south side of Missoula.
It has a pool table, a good country jukebox, and a
peremptorily amiable bartender, but by and large
the atmosphere is pretty businesslike, and the business at hand is alcohol. (THE DOCTOR IS IN AT SICKS

A.M. discreetly advises a small sign taped to the back-bar mirror.) The clientele is mostly trailer-court working class—day laborers and millhands and motel maids and Granny Goose salesmen and tire recappers and Korean War widows and Exxon pump jockeys—and it includes a sizable contingent of full-time, dedicated alcoholics.

Now, for all my inabstinent ways, I have never counted myself among that happy number; but when we lived in Missoula I did like to fall by the Elbow Room every now and then for a nightcap or three, just to clear my head after a hard day at the thesaurus or some trifling domestic impasse or a particularly egregious outrage on the late news. The glum, podiatrist's-waiting-room anonymity of the place seemed to cool me out somehow, and many's the midnight hour I've whiled away sitting there nursing a shot of Brand X bourbon and meditating upon the electric Hamm's Beer sign behind the bar, the one that bears the legend "Born in the Land of Sky-Blue Waters" beside an animated picture, which follows a rushing mountain stream down past a campsite with a red canoe, on down a riffle and over a waterfall and around an island and past a camp-site with a red canoe and down a riffle and over a waterfall and around an island and past a campsite with a red canoe and down a riffle and . . . The Hamm's sign, with that mad little river rushing eternally up its own fundament, has always seemed to me an ineffably profound representation of spiritual isolation, a sort of horizontal electric mandala for contemplative drunks, and I have long aspired to write a country song about it.

Why not now? Sure! I'll call it "Drowning in the Land of Sky-Blue Waters"; it'll be my personal anthem, an old honky-tonker's swan song. Within the next ten miles of freeway I've got the opening lines—"I've lost my way again / Out in this neon wilderness . . ."—and something that passes, at least to my tin ear, for a rudimentary tune. By lunchtime I have the first verse all wrapped up, and by our afternoon beer break, just across the Wyoming–Nebraska border, I've made it through the chorus. And before the sun goes down that evening, I am singing—if you can call it that—at the top of my inharmonious voice, the very first song I've ever written. No doubt there will be those who say that it should be the last as well, but that's *their* problem.

So, as Roy Rogers used to put it, "Now don't you worry, folks, we're a-gonna git them rustlers. But first, lemme sing ya a little song. It goes . . . kinda like this . . ."

I've lost my way again
Out in this neon wilderness,
Where the rivers run in circles
And the fish smoke cigarettes;

Where the only things that give me
Any peace of mind
Are a jukebox and a barstool
And a strange electric sign.

Drowning in the Land of Sky-Blue Waters

CHORUS:
'Cause I'm drowning in the land of sky-blue waters
Since I lost the way home to you.
Yes, I'm drowning in the land of sky-blue waters;
I need you to see me through.

I've seen that peaceful campsite
A hundred times tonight,
Where the campfire's always burning
And everything looks right.

But across that crazy river
In this godforsaken place,
A man is going under;
He could sink without a trace.

CHORUS:
For I'm drowning . . . (etc.)

The Elbow Room is closing now
And I must face the street,
Where the only rushing rivers
Are rivers of concrete.

There's no way I can cry for help;
My pride has got its rules.
But at last call for alcohol
My heart calls out to you:

CHORUS:
Oh, I'm drowning . . . (etc.)

As we roll on into the gathering Nebraska dark, I can feel the faint magnetic pull of all those honky-tonks out there, all the Dew Drop Inns in the Land of Doo-Wah-Diddie, neon lodestars in the night. But they're not for us, for our honky-tonkin' days are o'er—because although we won't even suspect it for weeks and weeks yet, when we pulled away from that nice motel this morning there was a stowaway among us, a tiny mite no bigger than the dot over the "i" in Sheridan. We must wait the requisite nine months before we get to look upon her darling face, and name her Annie June McClanahan. Our true collaboration has begun.

EIGHT

Tune Out, Turn In, Drop Off

All is ephemeral—fame and
the famous as well.

—MARCUS AURELIUS

LEST anyone suppose that I've exhausted my stock of Famous People stories, let me just point with pride to my former student the Low-Level Munchkin.

You don't remember the Low-Level Munchkin? She's that Reagan appointee—the one in the Easter Bunny suit—who got herself summarily dismissed from the Administration for turning in a report critical of her own employers' sexist hiring policies. Well, that Munchkin learned all she knows—not overmuch, evidently—in my creative-writing class, back when I still had my foot in the door at the Harvard of the West.

And did I mention that John Y. Brown, Jr., once bird-dogged my girlfriend? Or that I once guarded Cliff Hagan in a high school basketball game (everybody else on our team had the stomach flu) and held him to eleven points in three minutes of playing time? Or that Truman Capote once told me a joke? (This fella goes into a restaurant in New Orleans and asks for ham and eggs, and the waitress says, "Honey, I cain't give you no ham 'n' eggs this mornin'." "Why not?" he says. "Are you out of ham?" "No," she says, "we got plenty of ham." "Well, are you out of eggs?" "No, we got plenty of eggs." "Well then, why can't I have ham and eggs?" And she says, " 'Cause we ain't got no *grits*!") Or

181

that my mother lives across the street from Rosemary Clooney's brother? Or that Gay Brewer, Jr.,
once bird-dogged my girlfriend? (Same girlfriend
too. Was she trying to tell me something?) Or that
I once went roller-skating with the future daughter-
in-law of the former U.S. Senator from Nebraska?
Or that I happen to be personally acquainted with
the Condom King of Kingdom Come? Or that I once
had lunch with Robert Morley (and three hundred
other people) at the Four Seasons? (You don't believe me? I got pictures!) Or that, in 1953, I had a
blind date with the Top Parisian Fashion Model of
1957? Or that my friend Gurney Norman attended
the valedictory performance of Max Terhune and
His Talking Dummy in the World's Largest Fenced-
in Ballpark in Penington Gap, Virginia?

But all these reflected glories and twenty cents
will buy you a cup of instant coffee at the H&H
Coal Co. & Drug Store in Port Royal, Kentucky,
where I do a good deal of my socializing nowadays.
Port Royal's a nice little place; Cia and I have been
here almost ten years now, and it suits us fine. I
finally came to terms with that ancient nemesis, my
novel, a couple of years ago, and thanks in very
large measure to my late pard Little Enis, who
served as the inspiration for the novel's hero and
supplied some of its best lines, it turned out pretty
good. There was even a role in it for Old Blue; he
plays the Big Inch, and does the part (as it were)
with all the verve and panache we've come to know
and love him for. When the novel was published, I

got my name in *Newsweek*—and they spelled it wrong.

We haven't honky-tonked in years. My personal romance with country music ended the night I dropped by the Pit-Stop Bar & Bait Shop (formerly the M&M Disco & Bait Shop) for a beer and heard a song on the jukebox tenderly entitled "You Fuckin' Jerk, You Piss Me Off." I went home and wrote my own song, about a couple of drifters who find each other, fall in love, and come to rest in Kentucky. I'll spare you the rest of the lyrics this time, but the chorus goes . . . kinda like this:

All the roads in the world lead to home, sweet home;
They all lead the other way, too.
Some have to stay, and some have to go,
And some are just passin' through.

No more passin' through for us; we've finally found ourselves a place where the more things stay the same, the more they stay the same.

I do have one local Famous People story, though, about my neighbor and longtime dear friend Wendell Berry, celebrated poet, novelist, essayist, farmer, and ecology curmudgeon. When Wendell's *The Unsettling of America* was published a few years ago, his editor called one day, very excited, with the news that Robert Redford loved the book and was giving copies to all his friends for Christmas. Whereupon Wendell, as he hung up the phone, turned to his wife, Tanya, and said, "Queenie, who in the hell is Robert Redmon?"

Also, it seems to me that any reader who has persevered this far deserves to know that I owe my catfish dinner at the LBJ Ranch to the good offices of my estimable and amiable father-in-law, William S. White, who really *did* win a Pulitzer Prize.

And as I recall, I threatened, long ago, to bring Jimmy Sacca back onstage for one last encore—which entails another flashback, and yet another little one after that—and then I'll hush, and listen to *your* life story.

In the spring of the Long Hot Summer of 1964, when I was still an only slightly superannuated young Visiting Lecturer, the brightest and bravest of my students were making plans to put their ideals to the test that summer in Mississippi, registering voters. Naturally, there being no fool like an old fool, I got into my foolish old head the notion that I ought to go too, and said so out loud just often enough that, when the time came, I had to do it. So in August, during my annual visit to Kentucky, I borrowed a car and set out for Jackson, Mississippi. As usual, my timing was perfect: I left home less than a week after the bodies of Schwerner and Chaney and Goodman were discovered in a Mississippi mudbank. The following day, with my heart in my throat and my upper lip shaved clean and my ACLU membership card stashed under the floormat and my last roach flushed down the john of a Standard Oil station back in Memphis, Tennessee, I arrived in Jackson, to spearhead the civil-rights movement.

Well, for three days I couldn't even *find* the

damned civil-rights movement. I put up that first night in a nice, air-conditioned motel in downtown Jackson, not two blocks from the state capitol; as soon as I got my bearings, I figured, I'd move to more suitable quarters, possibly something in, say, a chicken coop behind a sharecropper's humble abode.

But that was before three straight afternoons of timorously cruising Jackson's steamy back streets, looking out of the corner of my eye for the outside-agitator headquarters. Each day I'd suit up in my voter registration outfit—starched khakis, wash 'n' wear button-down shirt, rep stripe tie—check out of the motel, and set forth into the heat and torpor in search of someone who could tell me what the hell I was supposed to do . . . and by three-thirty or four o'clock each afternoon, there I'd be, back in the motel swimming pool, spouting and wallowing in sweet relief. As far as I was ever able to determine, there wasn't a drop of alcohol for sale in all of Mississippi; I spent the evenings washing out my shirt and watching the civil-rights movement on the color TV in my air-conditioned room, while Ross Barnett snoozed like a babe just two blocks down the street.

On the fourth day, down to my last clean pair of khakis and running out of money fast, I finally stumbled, in my wanderings, upon outside-agitator central, the office of the Council of Federated Organizations, headquarters of the local voter registration effort. The place was swarming with college students proceeding purposefully about the business of the revolution; it was clear at a glance that they didn't have any openings for old fools, getting underfoot and taking up space in the chicken coop. I stumbled right back out again, sadder but wiser, and made for my motel; and in no time at all I was soothing my wounded pride in the cool, refreshing waters of the swimming pool.

That evening, in celebration of my retirement as kingpin of the civil-rights movement and my imminent departure from Jackson and all its no doubt charming environs, I took myself to a downtown theater and treated me to the new Tennessee Williams movie, *The Night of the Iguana*. Afterward, I took a walk around the business district, at ease on Jackson's streets for the first time since I'd come to town, no longer a cringing carpetbagger. So I was ambling along, musing on the sense of humor of a God so waggish He'd book Tennessee Williams and Ross Barnett into town on the same night, when I rounded a corner and was much taken aback to see, two or three doors down the block, a large neon sign proclaiming:

JIMMY SACCA'S

RESTAURANT

Picture this: a medium-sized, medium-nice Southern café, paneled in knotty pine, booths along the wall and tables in the middle; there's a lunch counter, and a steam table, upon which is mounted the ubiquitous varnished *hammus alabammus*, turning on a spit beneath an infrared light. The walls behind the counter and above the booths are decorated with framed, signed photographs bearing such legends as "Good luck in your new venture, Jim! Your pal, Vic Damone" and "Best wishes to a great Kentuckian! Sincerely, Lt. Gov. 'Doc' Beauchamp" and "Dear Jimmie, love ya, Diana Dors" and "Best of luck to a grand guy, yours truly, Phil Harris." Some are glossies of Sacca himself, alone or with Billy Vaughn and the rest of the Hilltoppers, wearing the trademark Hilltopper regalia of their heyday— WKSTC letter sweaters and freshman beanies and bow ties. Near the cash register is an immense jukebox, gaudy but silent. It's getting on toward closing time; there are two couples lingering over coffee in separate booths, and an old lady is administering the last rites to a Salisbury steak at a table near the door. Behind the steam table, under a blackboard that announces "Today's Special, Roast Beef with Au Jus, 2 Veg., $1.95," stands a solitary waitress, stolidly chewing gum, her arms folded. And sitting at the counter, wearing a long white apron and reading the sports page of the Jackson newspaper is . . .

Jimmy Sacca.

I'd have known him anywhere. He'd put on a few pounds all right, and he was wearing glasses, and where the beanie used to sit I detected what could be the beginning of a bald spot. But there was no mistaking that Ramon Novarro profile: the hooded eyes, the noble Roman hooter; inside this well-fed Italian gent in the apron was Jimmy Sacca, teen idol. Alas, poor Sacca; I knew him when.

I took a seat at the counter, a few stools from his. He was checking the race results, and he didn't look up when I sat down.

"If you was wanting the roast beef, hon," the waitress bawled from her post by the steam table, "we ain't got no more Aw Juice."

No thanks, I told her; I'd just have a cup of coffee. While she brought it, I flipped through the offerings on the Select-O-Matic affixed to the countertop before me; sure enough, among the selections was a whole bank of vintage Hilltopper tunes. I fished a dime from my pocket and punched "From the Vine Came the Grape"—possibly because it had the highest alcohol content of anything I'd come across in Jackson—and Sacca's sweet, lugubrious tenor filled the room: "From the vine came the grape, from the grape came the wine . . ." Sacca glanced up, favored me with the tiniest smile in the history of mirth, and turned his attention back to the morning line at Hialeah.

Nonetheless, by the time the song arrived at its perfervid conclusion—"My bella Maria, you're mi-i-i-ine!"—I was ready with one of my patented snappy opening lines of celebrity repartee. "Uh, Mr. Sacca," I blurted into the ensuing silence, "you probably don't remember me, but . . ."

Sacca lowered his paper and looked at me over

the top of his spectacles. "Nope," he admitted, not impolitely, "can't say I do."

"Well, I'm a Kentuckian too, and . . ."

"That a fact? I come from Lockport, New York, myself."

". . . and, uh, I sort of met you one time in, uh, Bowling Green at the Manhattan Towers in 1952, I think it was; you were with Billy Vaughn and I was with a guy named Riley, uh, Walter Riley, you might remember him, he was Mr. Freshman Personality of BGBU, red-headed guy, Walter Riley? So anyhow, uh, we . . ."

"That a fact?" said Sacca, refolding his paper to the funnies as my voice trailed off to nowhere. "Well, there's a lot of water has gone over the bridge since then, a lot of water."

I saw, at last, that he'd just as soon I did my reminiscing on my own time. Alas, poor Sacca; he'd put in a long evening back there behind the steam table, up to his elbows in Aw Juice, and now he just wanted to rest his dogs and read the funnies. Fame, it is written, is a wart—and right now Sacca was the fame, I the wart. There was one other stratagem I might have tried . . . but I was, after all, a grown man now, and a certified Visiting Lecturer in Creative Writing, and somehow I just couldn't quite bring myself to ask him for his autograph.

Instead, by way of a more subtle tribute, I plugged the Select-O-Matic with a quarter, good for three more numbers from the Hilltopper hit parade. Dur-

ing "P.S., I Love You" the couple in the front booth
paid their check and left, and before "I'd Rather
Die Young" was halfway over, the other couple had
gone too. The old lady was bidding a fond farewell
to her last morsel of Salisbury steak, and Sacca had
finished the funnies and turned to the front page.
GOV. BARNETT SAYS "NEVER!" screamed the headline,
above a photo of that enlightened public servant,
plump and balding, shaking his fist like a bellicose
oyster in a seersucker suit.

"Ol' Ross," Sacca chuckled, as the record changed.
"He's a hairpin, ain't he?" It was an assessment of
the governor with which, happily, even a big-time
civil-rights leader such as myself need have no argument. "Better drink up on your coffee, pal," my host
advised me. "It's time to pull the sidewalks in."

"I-hi-hi-hi'm trying to fore-getchew," warbled the
Sacca on the jukebox, "but try as I ma-a-ay . . ."

My coffee cup was empty. "Well, so long, Mr.
Sacca," I said, rising to go. "It was nice seeing you
. . . again."

"Yeah, great, great," he said absently. "Hurry
back, now."

"No use trying to forget you . . ." the jukebox
Sacca tearfully averred, as I slouched out the door.

And on that resoundingly anticlimactic note this
story ought, properly, to end, for from that moment
to this I've not crossed paths again with Jimmy
Sacca. There is—I admit it—nothing further to
report; I went back to the motel, I went back to

Kentucky, I went back to California . . . and so, on; and so, forth. If you've read this far, you know the rest.

But I hate to leave Jimmy Sacca that way, sitting there in his dirty apron in Jackson, Mississippi, with his memories pinned to the walls around him like so many desiccated butterflies. Better we remember a warm spring night of long ago, a crescent moon, a starry sky, an old brick dormitory on a quiet college campus. Now, out of the shadows, a car creeps almost silently up the driveway, headlights off, and glides to a stop before the dorm. A figure emerges from the car, a male, tall and broad-shouldered. It's Jimmy Sacca! He moves stealthily across the lawn, plants himself in a shaft of moonlight beneath a certain window, raises his arms, and—

But what's this? For now two more figures have left the car and joined Sacca on the lawn. At his left is Billy Vaughn, and hard by his right is—yes!—it's Ned McManahan! There we are in our WKSTC letter sweaters and our bow ties and beanies, there we are, Hilltoppers all, raising our arms in unison and lifting our voices in golden harmony: *"I-hi-hi-hi'm trying to forget you . . ."* In the window above us a light comes on, and framed in the lighted square is not just some anonymous cutie in pincurls, but—yes! yes!—the Dairy Princess of Menifee County, her form divine filmed in the sheerest of pink gossamer negligees. *"But try-y-y*

191

as I ma-a-ay . . ." we keen, our arms outstretched, our voices all as one: *"You're still my every thought, dear, / Every day . . ."*

Then, like a veil from our eyes, the entire third dimension drops away around us—from the crescent moon in the starry sky, from the quiet campus and the dorm and the lighted window, even from the Dairy Princess of Menifee County—and leaves us at the center of a vast, empty stage before a painted backdrop, under a paper moon. *"No use trying to forget you, / 'Cause I realize . . ."* The shaft of moonlight has become a spotlight's blinding beam, at our feet blaze ranks of footlights, and in the measureless void beyond them is an audience as big as all of Western Civilization. *". . . That I'm trying to forget you / With teardrops in my eyes . . ."*

Our faces wreathed in smiles, the bloom of youth upon our cheeks, our single voice pealing like a crystal carillon, we reach the final chorus of our song:

"Now I know I haven't a chance, dear / There's no denying . . ."—in perfect synchronicity we execute a nimble half-step forward and touch our right hands to our hearts and extend our left hands to the audience—*"But you can't blame a fel-low for try-ing!"*

We doff our beanies and take our bows, as waves of applause wash over us. For we're the Hilltoppers, we're Sacca and Vaughn and McWhat's-His-Name, and we're . . . famous!

CURTAIN CALL

Now let's hear it for some of the wonderful folks who made this show possible.

For K.C., the Lord High Mayor of Skylonda, and for Danny, the Grand Tabboon of Mizzoo, a coupla swell fellas; for Wendell and Tanya and Jim and Mary Ann and Gurney and Jim and Michele, dear friends and splendid listeners all; for Nedro and Deb, the Perfect Hosts; for Bobbie Mason, the known world's foremost Hilltopper authority; for Kit, who lived most of these chapters too; for Perry Lane Jane, the original Life of the Party; for Fred "Front Page" Nelson and his hair-trigger tape recorder; for my sweet boys Jess and Bill; for Enis's own Barbara and Donna Faye, a pair of peaches, and for Pat Madden, who loved the old boy like a brother; for Jim and Lois Welch, who throw a mean cocklety factail party; for th' whole gang at the Raucous Raftin' Ruckus; for my peerless pal Guy Mendes, whose photographs of Enis win the Ned McManahan Good Art award in a walk; for Bill and June and Ron and Vicky, in-laws *par excellence*; for Fletcher and Barbara Vick, who made Boots' Bar everything it had to be, and then some; for Messrs. Stegner and Scowcroft and Cowley and Summers and Hazel and Havighurst, gratefully, and for Bill Jansen, the one I owe him; for Stan and Den, the nick-o'-time kids; for Bob Stone, who held

195

Paul Newman down for me while I ordained him;
for Kevin "Flash" Flood, who led us to the lair of
the wily Pisswilliger; for R. C. Kohler and his Moon-
pie, who showed us more of Albuquerque than we
probably needed to know; for Joe Lomax, who
steered us through the midnight wilds of Houston,
and brought us in without a scratch; for a certain
beefy, red-faced Irishman I once thought I knew;
for Ken and Faye, with love and wonder; and for
Elizabeth McKee, matchless agent and honored
friend, with an armful of red, red roses.

And a special tip of the McClanahat to Rust Hills
and Joy Williams, who in 1974 invited me to a cocktail party at which were Norman Mailer and Kurt
Vonnegut and George Plimpton and Hortense Cali-
sher and the novelist Brock Brower and his wife
Anne, the former future Top Parisian Fashion
Model of 1957, with whom I'd had that blind date
in 1953, and whom I'd last seen in 1961 at another
cocktail party at which were Saul Bellow and Robert
Lowell and Edward Albee and . . .

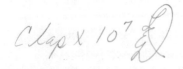